60 WAYS TO HURRAY!

RALPH VARCOE

Copyright © 2019 Ralph Varcoe

All rights reserved.

ISBN: 978-1-78972-216-1

For E, P, A, C, and M.

From 'This girl can' to 'These girls do'.

CONTENTS

	Acknowledgments	i
	Introduction	1
	Getting to Hurray is Easier than you Think	3
	The FEDAMP Productivity Model	5
1	Focus	7
2	Efficiency	45
3	Distraction	75
4	Action	99
5	Motivation	115
6	Person	127
7	What Next?	161
8	Can you do me a Favour?	163
9	More at Accelerate Performance	165
	About the Author	167

ACKNOWLEDGMENTS

Huge thanks to all the amazing people I've worked with over the years. I have learned something valuable from every single one of you.

The biggest thank you, though, goes to Emma, for everything.

INTRODUCTION

Welcome to 60 Ways to Hurray!

This book is designed to help you on your journey to becoming a seriously productive ninja! There are actually 67 ideas contained in the 6 sections of the FEDAMP Productivity Model, but the title seemed better with a round number! So, there are 7 bonus items, just for you.

I've spent a long time in business, having run my own and worked for a number of global corporates. When I started out I was super inefficient with my time and not very good at focusing on the really important stuff. As I progressed I realised I could get more done if I was a bit more organised and made sure the really important things got done first.

Achieving goals is a bit of a drug. Every time something is completed there's a little 'reward high'. It became fun.

There's a lot of information you can research out there that points to how you can become more productive, but it is all a bit haphazard.

60 Ways to Hurray! brings together a lot of really sound suggestions and puts them into a simple model, focusing

on 6 key areas; Focus, Efficiency, Distraction, Action, Motivation, and Person.

I hope you find some of this thought provoking and useful.

If any of it helps you accelerate towards your goals then please share your stories at:
accelerate-performance.com/feedback60
or email me at info@accelerate-performance.com

GETTING TO HURRAY! IS EASIER THAN YOU THINK

What do I mean by getting to Hurray? Just that 'Hurray' is what we say or shout when something good happens. When someone accomplishes something, or has good news. When what they wanted comes true.

In 60 Ways to Hurray! we'll help you achieve your goals fast by implementing some awesome productivity tips. In achieving your goals, I sincerely hope you, your friends and family will be whooping "Hurray!" when you get what you set out to achieve.

Don't think you need to implement all 67 tips. Even I don't do them all. The most important thing is to find the ones that work for you and then do them so regularly that they become habits. Habits are such useful autopilots (assuming they're good ones!). Set them up and let them carry you to your greatness.

There are some tips which I think are more fundamental than others, such as defining your goals, writing them down, breaking them down into sub-goals, and taking action. Without those there's little point in looking at the efficiency tips or motivation.

Being more Efficient and eliminating Distractions will help you Focus and take Action. Your Motivation is what'll keep you going when the going gets tough. And the Person at the centre of all of it needs to be looked after and managed so that good things happen without burn-out.

My advice is to rank your top 3 from each section of the FEDAMP Productivity Model and implement them today. Over the next weeks and months gradually introduce some more. Assess which ones are working for you and stop those that aren't helping. Replace them with others that might.

But, be sure you've given yourself enough time to establish the ones you choose as a habit before ditching anything.

THE FEDAMP PRODUCTIVITY MODEL

Throughout my working life I've tried to find ways of becoming more efficient and effective at what I'm doing. As I researched various tried and tested productivity 'hacks' I realised that a lot of advice out there is sound but not really structured. There's lots of stuff about goal setting and time management, as well as other things mixed in, but it's all a bit hit and miss.

I felt that it would be more powerful to structure these great ideas into a model that logically breaks down the tips into 6 categories.

1. Focus
2. Efficiency
3. Distraction
4. Action
5. Motivation
6. Person

This is the FEDAMP Productivity Model.

The most important of the 6 are Focus and Action. Without taking Action there is no forward movement. Without Focus there is no map of where you're going. Taking Action without knowing where you're going is a really pointless exercise, resulting in wasted resources, time, and energy. It will lead to significant frustration.

Efficiency is about taking the things you do today and making better use of your time in doing them. Why take 2 hours over something that could take 20 minutes, if only you knew better how to do it more efficiently?

Distraction is about eliminating or, at the very least, minimising the things that seek to divert your laser focus.

Motivation is all about what keeps you driving forwards when things get a bit slow, hard, and boring.

And, finally, Person is about you and what can help you feel better, happier, and healthier as you achieve something utterly amazing.

Mapping these 67 ideas into these 6 categories makes it simple to know where to focus for what aim.

You could argue that where I've categorised them isn't quite right for you. That's OK. This isn't about whether I've got it right, it's about putting down a framework and then looking to see which best fits where. If you think something shouldn't be in Efficiency but it should be in Focus, that's fine. This is all about what works for you and how it helps you deliver on your ambitions a bit faster than you would have done if you hadn't read this book.

Remember that you now have a choice - rather than being Fed-Up with not achieving much at all, you can flip that for FEDAMP and be a productive badass! And who doesn't what to be one of them?

1 FOCUS

There are two key things about Focus: Defining the end point, and Taking steps towards getting there. If you don't have both of these then you aren't going to 'deliberately' achieve much at all. You might accidentally do something brilliant, discover something that changes the world, or become an overnight sensation. But for every person who is an accidental achiever, there are millions who didn't get so lucky.

Define the end point:

"If you don't know where you're going how do you know when you've got there?"

What does success look like? What will you have done? Achieved? How will you know when you've reached the end? It is critical to define what you're trying to do and to be clear about what you will have as evidence. Be as specific as possible. Will you have a book available for sale to the public, will you have the medal for completing the marathon, will you have your first paying customer, or the 15 ringing endorsements you desire for your new product?

Taking Steps:

"If you don't move in the direction you are wanting to go then you'll never get there."

You have to take action. No point sitting in a car with the engine off, your SatNav telling you it'll take 2h43m to drive the 181 miles to your destination and just hoping somehow, you'll arrive. It sounds obvious but the key to success is staying focused on the things that get you to where you want to be. Taking action is dealt with in more detail in 3. but for now, stay focused on what you need to do to take those steps towards your goals.

1.1 Write, Write, Write. Right?

How much can you remember? Have you played that game where you get shown a heap of things on a table or tray and you have to remember as many as you can after only looking at it for a minute or so? There used to be a game show on British TV called "The Generation Game" in which contestants had to memorise the items on a conveyor belt and then win them if they could recall what they were. There was always a cuddly toy!

How many things can you remember in a game like that? (Can you even remember playing the game?).

I sometimes find it hard to remember what happened yesterday because life is so full and busy.

I attend meetings and am amazed that some people bring a note book but barely open it to take notes. I used to be super impressed that their memory was awesome, and a little bit jealous that it was clearly better than mine.

Only, it wasn't! Guaranteed that a week later I'd ask them about a specific point from the meeting they wrote no notes in and they hadn't the foggiest idea. I, on the other hand, knew. Why?

Because I'd written it all down.

Make notes. Make more notes. Write it all down because unless you are someone with an eidetic memory (photographic) you're going to forget some of it.

And bad news for those of us getting a bit older…..it gets worse. So, keep copious notes. Always.

1.2 Plan, Goals and Deadlines

Now you're in the habit of writing it all down you can start to keep your plans, goals and deadlines in your journal.

It doesn't matter whether you keep your notes and plans electronically or manually. What matters is that you keep them.

If you have an idea about what you want to achieve but you don't write it down what is likely to happen? You'll forget it. It will fade to becoming a nice to do but it won't stay front of mind. Even if you do remember it, you won't necessarily stick to it because you can kind of adapt it as you go and won't notice because you never set the map's coordinates. The inevitable scope creep will mean you end up in Scarborough rather than Blackpool.

You need to write your goals down. Make them concrete. Make them a real thing. Commit yourself to paper and remind yourself what you're aiming for.

Then you need to write down the process steps that will get you to your goal. These are the actionable steps that move you towards the ultimate goal.

When I announced to a very surprised family that I was going to run the London Marathon I could have just written that big hairy goal down and dreamed of achieving it. But since their surprise was due to the fact I could barely run a bath, I had to define process steps along the way.

I had to buy the right shoes, establish a training plan, stick to the plan, enter some shorter races in preparation, change my routine, change my diet, plan for recovery times, and so on. All of these process steps were actionable little goals along the path to getting the medal.

Lastly, every goal needs a deadline attached. When are you planning to do it? In the case of the Marathon it was easy…..it's on a specific date in April. I just had to work backwards and fill in the process steps with dates to enable me to get there uninjured and physically fit enough to participate without needing medical attention.

We'll look at why adding deadlines is a golden tip later. But for now, write your goals down, plan your process steps and give each one a deadline.

This will be the map which you'll refer to over and over again.

1.3 Three Most Important Things

Before you go to bed at night, write down the three most important tasks you need to achieve the next day. Don't wait until you wake up a bit spaced out with the day-to-day stresses of getting kids up, the commute, or the horror of the news programmes (more on news later!).

Be really clear about what is going to move you forwards and then rank them. Pick the top three and these become your immediate To Dos in the morning.

Your list may have a dozen things on it, but it's the top three that you need to focus on.

How do you decide what the most important tasks are? In section 1.6 Important or Urgent we look at how to evaluate which the highest priority tasks are.

Once you have your top three written down, you can go to bed clear in the knowledge that you have a plan set. As you sleep soundly your subconscious can get to work helping you complete them relatively quickly when you wake.

The next morning, clear of distractions, set about completing those three tasks before you tackle anything else.

Imagine the feeling once you've ticked them off. Tasks that are moving you substantially closer to achieving your goals. Everything else that day will feel like icing on top of a really fine cake.

Now imagine you leave them and don't tackle them in the morning. It's getting to the afternoon and you're a little tired from the day, in need of a pick-you-up. These three things are still hanging over you. You're no further towards your goal but you feel like you've been really busy, nonetheless. You try to tackle them that evening and manage only one and a bit. You fall asleep wishing you'd been a bit more organised with a lot of regret, feeling overwhelmed.

I know which one I'd rather feel.

Get the three most important things defined before you sleep. Then tackle them first.

1.4 How to Concentrate Better

In Section 3, Distraction we'll look at how to avoid as many distractions as possible in order that you can focus. But assuming you are of a mind-set to do some really good work, what's the best way to concentrate and get stuff done efficiently?

The human brain can't concentrate effectively for very long, sustained periods of time. It depends on which studies you look at but it's thought that maximum concentration is anywhere from 25-45 minutes. This means that while you can still concentrate after this time is up (else how can we sit a 3 hour exam or drive 5 hours straight) your peak levels of concentration tail off and you become less effective.

It's not just about concentration. It's also about creativity and mental alertness. These diminish over time too. It stands to reason, therefore, that if you give yourself some breaks to zone out and refresh, the quality of your work will be higher for longer.

Take the example of someone writing for 3 hours at a time. Say their normal hourly word rate is 2,000. In 3 hours straight they may get only 4,300 words written as their productivity tails off.

Then take the example of someone who works and rests in short bursts. A total of 2 hours 20 minutes working and 40 minutes at rest. They achieve 4,800 words. The quality is more consistent and better. They feel more energetic and less drained.

Interval working is good for you, just like interval training is for physical fitness.

1. Select the task
2. Set a timer for 25 minutes and work solidly with no distraction for that duration
3. Take a 5 minute break. Get up. Walk around. Zone out.
4. Set a timer for 25 minutes and work solidly with no distraction for that duration
5. Take a 5 minute break. Get up. Walk around. Zone out.
6. Repeat steps 2-5
7. Take a longer break of 20 minutes
8. And repeat from step 2

This technique was made famous by using a timer in the shape of a red tomato and is most commonly referred to as the Pomodoro Technique (Pomodoro is Italian for tomato).

There are plenty of Apps out there to help. Or go low tech and get a regular kitchen timer (tomato shape not necessary!)

1.5 Just Say 'No'

You cannot do everything. No matter how efficient you become, you just can't. None of us can.

You know what they say? "If you want something done, ask a busy person". If you're a busy and efficient person who gains a reputation for getting things done people will probably gravitate to asking you to take on more. Organising the school quiz night, another extra-curricular project at work, or being the coordinator for the local neighbourhood watch.

You should always ask yourself how many of these extra things are your priority? If one or more of them are on your goal list then take them on and do them amazingly well. But if they aren't then they are distractions. These extra things will take your time and rob that oh-so-precious and finite commodity.

It may not come naturally to you, especially if you are typically a 'people pleaser', but you need to learn to say "NO" to things that don't move you towards your goals. Why would you take on a task that is someone else's priority if it's not aligned with your own? It just doesn't make sense.

"But," I hear you cry, "I'm part of a community and have friends who I want to help. I want to have and maintain relationships with them. So I need to do things for them."

Yes and no. It absolutely is right to be there for friends and family and to take things on for them, if appropriate. But, you must evaluate whether someone else can do them instead, depending on the time you have available.

If you're naturally used to saying yes it's going to feel really unnatural to say no. You may feel guilty. Just go with it, because this is about focusing on your goals, and while you're doing that, to give yourself the time to drive towards your goals, other things will need to give.

Get used to saying no. Do it the next time you're asked to take something extra on (unless it fits with your goals).

All you need to say is, "I'm really sorry but I can't do that right now as I'm up against a deadline on some work". That's true - your work! Your goals. An investment in your future.

1.6 Important or Urgent

Eisenhower was the 34th President of the United States. He served as a General in the second world war and was the first Supreme Commander of NATO. He knew a thing or two about what was important and what was urgent.

He came up with a simple model that enables you to determine if a task is important, urgent, both, or neither. He suggested how to handle each of the four categories.

- **Important** and **Urgent**: Do straight away
- **Important** but Not Urgent: Schedule (and spend most of your time here)
- Not Important but **Urgent**: Delegate
- Not Important and Not Urgent: Eliminate

The definition of Important is, well, important here. Something that goes into this category is one that moves you forward towards your goal. It's something like 'research the topic for my book', or 'run the 16km training run to build stamina'. These are what get you to where you want to be.

Urgent is something that has a time dependency and a consequence of not doing. Filing your tax return by 31st January (if you've not already done it) is urgent to avoid penalties. Someone telling you a report is needed as they have to brief their manager today is urgent.

Things that are not urgent include checking Facebook, chatting to your co-worker about their cat, or updating your Instagram feed. These are also almost definitely not important either.

Ideally nothing is in category 1 because you're on top of what needs to get done so things have not become urgent. Work to get these under control first.

Category 2 is where you want to focus most of your energy - on the tasks that drive things forwards.

If it's not important to you but it is urgent see if you can find someone else who could do it, for whom this may be important. Ideally you want to delegate as much of these items as possible. There will be some times when you can't (your boss needs something urgently and you're the only one with the information) and you'll just need to go with it.

And if something is nether important to you, nor urgent, just bin it. Who cares if it is ever done? No-one. Eliminate these distractions.

1.7 Use Your Alphabet

Another way of looking at your tasks is to use your ABCDE.

It's really simple. Rank the tasks according to the below categories:

    A tasks = The most important
    B tasks = The second most important
    C tasks = The third most important
    D tasks = Delegate
    E tasks = Eliminate

D tasks are equivalent to Not Important but Urgent. E tasks are equivalent to Not Important and Not Urgent. Your As are likely to be your Important and Urgents. And the BCs are a two tier list for the area you want to spend most of your time in.

Personally I find this approach less useful than the Eisenhower methodology as that forces you to think hard about the importance and the urgency and then categorise.

But if this approach works for you, use it. It's all about what makes you more effective and keeps you focused on your goals.

1.8 Get Someone Else to Do It

In the previous sections 1.6 and 1.7 we talked about delegating your urgent but not important tasks.

It's really easy to say that but how do you do it in practice?

Remember how we talked about a sense of guilt when saying "No" to people because you may naturally be a people pleaser, or just used to saying yes. You're probably going to feel a similar level of guilt about getting someone else to do the thing, whatever that is.

There are three ways of getting someone else to do the task:

1. It is their job anyway

    Imagine you are asked to put together a report for your boss giving an overview of what your sales team has been up to. You could build this all yourself from what you know already and ring around the team to get their updates, or you can provide them a template and get them to fill it in.

Your job is to consolidate it or better still, given you are becoming a delegation god(ess), ask one of the team to consolidate it for you. It's already the team members' job to update you so why not get them to do all the hard work for the report?

2. You appeal to someone's good nature

You have a deadline for your work (your work/your goal) and this other, now urgent, thing needs to happen too. Can your spouse or partner do it for you? Would your friend be able to do it instead? Most people are happy to do favours for each other but it is a two-way street, so remember that when you do have time you can offer to do something for them, even unprompted (see Section 6.5 for more ideas on this).

3. You pay someone

Your friend or partner is unlikely to want do your tax return for you. But your accountant can. It'll cost you but this specialist help will ensure it is done right and on time, leaving you with the time to focus on what's important for you.

Always ask someone politely and with good grace. Don't demand they do it for you. Don't tell them you want them to do it because it's not important to you (how great would that make them feel?).

Do let them know that you would do it but have some pressing commitments that you need to complete, but this other thing needs to be done and ask if they would do you a favour.

Then, at some point in the not very distant future, do something unexpected and helpful for them.

You'll be surprised. Most people are only too happy to help. If you ask nicely.

1.9 One Fifth is the Magic Number

One fifth of 100 is 20. What's so special about that number?

Vilfredo Pareto noticed in 1896 that almost 80% of the land in Italy was owned by only 20% of the population. Subsequent studies have shown that this ratio is fairly constant in many things.

The top 20% of customers generate 80% of the revenues of a company. The wealth is distributed in a similar fashion, and so on. In reality, whether it is 80/20, 70/30 or 90/10, the principle holds true.

Management consultants have looked into this phenomenon as well and concluded that 80% of results come from 20% of the input. Basically there is a law of diminishing returns on further effort (refer back to 1.4 where we talked about concentration).

If this is true, and a lot of research says that it broadly is, then only 1/5th of your inputs will result in the greatest returns.

This is why you need to focus on the most important tasks first (section 1.3, 1.6, 1.7) in order to drive the most significant gains as quickly as possible.

Be relentless about which inputs you focus on that really drive you towards achieving your goals. Avoid the distractions and concentrate hard. These most important tasks are the 20% and, by being laser focused, you can achieve 80% relatively quickly.

1.10 When to Take Action

The time to take action is once you are sure the action is related to a smart goal.

You've written your Goals down (1.2) and you've broken these down into smaller process goals, each one aligned to getting you to success. Each one of these process steps must also be smart, or SMART.

If you're really new to this sort of thing you might not know what SMART means though I suspect many of you will.

S = Specific

Make sure the goal isn't vague like 'read around my topic'. How do you know when you've achieved that and how do you know that it's getting you to gold? A goal like "Read academic papers relating to dragonfly migrations during leap years" is much more specific.

M = Measurable

How many academic papers? Not giving something measurable means you don't know when you've completed it. "Read 6 academic papers relating to dragonfly migrations during leap years" is better.

A = Achievable (or Agreed upon if in a group. It should still be achievable, nevertheless)

Are there enough academic papers relating to dragonflies that you can read? If only one has ever been written then setting a goal for reading 6 is unachievable and it fails the SMART criteria test.

R = Realistic

Are you able to do it? Do you have the resources, time, and access to be able to do it? If you were to set a goal of "Pilot a helicopter to Middle-Earth" you'd fail the SMART test (everyone knows Helicopters aren't allowed there!) You'll also fail if you don't have a flying licence.

T = Time-bound

What's the deadline? If your goal of reading the dragonfly papers is open ended then you may never finish it. What's compelling you to complete it? There really isn't any point setting a goal without a timeframe. A goal without a due date is just a dream.

Once you know your actions are SMART the time to take action is NOW. We'll look more at starting in section 4.3.

1.11 Capture and Bottle Them

Ever had a brilliant idea or a fleeting thought and said to yourself I must remember that later? It is genius. It's going to form the basis of your new product idea, or it'll help make the daily work updates more easily automated, or maybe it'll be the start of a premise for the new book you're itching to write.

But do you remember them all? I know I don't. If I had £1 for every time I'd had a flash of what I thought was brilliance, only to forget it, I'd be a bit better off than I am today. The reason I wouldn't be a Millionaire is because I'm not brilliant enough to have loads of amazing ideas. But when I do have them I really regret not being able to recall what I wanted to do.

Once you're in the habit of writing, writing, and writing everything down (1.1) you will easily be able to jot down these ideas as they come to you.

I recall watching a programme about Michael McIntyre who in 2012 was the highest grossing comedian in the world. He's a naturally funny man but he doesn't just stand on stage being funny without any preparation. He keenly observes the world around him and turns things that strike him as funny into his very animated stage show. And wherever he goes he writes stuff down, even on a napkin if he doesn't have a notebook.

Imagine how much less material he'd have to make us laugh if he tried to remember everything and didn't write it down.

Here's another analogy. Think of yourself as the Big Friendly Giant, Roald Dahl's creation from the book 'The BFG'. He would catch dreams and put them in jars in order that he could blow them into the bedrooms of children.

Go and capture your dreams. Put them on paper. But do not attempt to blow them into bedrooms! You may get arrested.

1.12 List Your Projects

This tip is simple. Create lists of your projects and actions.

Write a separate list for every project with the key action points or process steps that will enable you to achieve the big goals. The action points are like waypoints on your journey. All you have to think about is getting to the next waypoint. You can stop thinking about the long distance, or how much work there is to do. It's just a nice little step along the way.

Focusing on one point in the list at a time and making that your next focus means you move forwards and stop worrying about the big stuff.

To take this waypoint-by-waypoint approach means you need to be really clear about the steps you're going to need to complete to get there. You have to map them all out. Plan in great detail so that all bases are covered.

You need to feel like you're joining the dots of the To Do list, and eventually a picture emerges.

It seems simple, and it is. But there's a lot of thought that goes in to putting a complete list together.

Start with the end in mind and then define the process steps to build on each other towards the ultimate goal.

I tend to write lists everywhere and for everything, so I don't forget. And so I know what little step I need to take next.

And then, once I've completed things I tick the items off one by one. A big fat tick if it's on paper or green colour in a cell on Excel. Either way I make it obvious and clear that I've made progress.

Once I've ticked something off I simply move on.

1.13 Create Systems

There are some tasks that we all have to do regularly. Others are similar in nature.

Say you're a writer or blogger and one of your goals is to write 3-5 blog posts a week, each of 500-600 words. Each one of the posts needs to be about something your readership will be interested in.

While the topics for each post may be different, there are lots of things that are the same or similar. Let's break them down:

- Decide on topic area
- Research topic
- Find 3 good references
- Write an introduction
- Tell a story about how the topic has been applied
- Suggest how the reader can benefit from it
- Engage with the readership
- Promote a call to action

- Write a title that's eye-catching
- Find an appropriate image
- SEO optimise the post
- Publish the post
- Add post to social media schedule app

This process is going to be broadly the same for every post so it would be really useful to have a checklist that ensures consistency every time a post is written and published.

You can do this in other areas of your life too. Practically all areas. Study what you do on a daily basis that's routine, where things are repeated. Then define the steps that are taken and turn these into your system for completing that task.

The more systems you have the more things will become habitual and the easier it will be to complete your goals or other daily tasks.

1.14 Bin the Swiss Army Knife Approach

A Swiss Army Knife is a real wonder tool. The Daddy of all multi-tools that makes a Leatherman look impoverished by comparison.

The array of tools is vast. Who knew there was such a thing to get stones out of hooves, or one to undo shackle pins? If you look hard enough you'll find a bread maker, I'm sure. It's brilliant. Why lug a toolbox with you when one admittedly rather bulky knife thing will turn you into a superhero.

Only, here's the thing. While it can do about a thousand different things it can't do more than one at a time. Try unscrewing something at the same time as filing your nails. Or cutting a piece of paper while sawing a dowelling rod. Useless. Utterly useless.

It's the same for us. We are just a big walking, talking version. Only a lot smarter.

Now before you attempt to prove how smart you are by telling me that we can all multi-task like a boss because we can eat, blink, breathe and watch EastEnders at the same time, these aren't multi-tasks. They are all autopilot functions. Even watching EastEnders!

And then there are those who will say "Paff…..only someone who doesn't have a family could possibly suggest that life can be anything other than a multi-tasking hell!" I have a family and, for a man (let's get that stereotype out there as well while we're at it!), am as able to help with homework, cook a meal, attend a conference call, and polish the silver, as the next person.

But it won't be the best meal I've ever cooked. I won't have heard/listened to everything that went on during the call. I may well have made a mistake in year 6 maths homework. And the silver won't be as shiny as it could have been had I been giving it my full attention.

It's not to say that multi-tasking isn't a necessary evil. But it is to say that if you want to drive a particular goal hard then you need to get on the monorail and do one thing and one thing only while you're doing it.

In experiments conducted in 2001, scientists looked at the time cost of switching between tasks. Moving between even fairly basic tasks showed it took longer to complete a set compared to a control group. When the tasks got more complex the group switching between tasks took even longer. The scientists concluded that even brief mental blocks resulting from shifts between tasks can waste up to 40% of productive time.

If you are serious about focusing on completing your goal then why not give yourself that 40% back by eliminating every other task while you're doing it. Do just one thing and make it count.

Multi-tasking for anyone who wants to accelerate their success is a seriously bad idea.

1.15 Weekly One-to-One

If you're managing a team of people at work you will need to monitor their progress. After all, you'll have to report upwards on how they, and you, are doing. At the start of the year you'll have set some broad goals for them. They will have specific goals that tell them what's expected of them.

Your job as a manager is to keep track of what's going on, where they need help, what they are doing well and where they can offer support to others in the team. You'll use all of this information to work out a coaching plan. You'll find the right 3rd party mentor who can help them develop professionally and personally so their career can move forward.

So often I hear managers say, "I know what they are up to, as we speak every day, and I'm in the detail of their jobs with them. I don't need a formal one-to-one with them. We're aligned."

Wrong. The one-to-one is a way of stepping back and evaluating whether the direction of travel towards the goals is right, what help and support they need, if there's training needed, and what coaching/mentoring would be useful.

When you set your own goals for your personal or professional ambitions you automatically become your own manager. It is your job to hold the same one-to-ones to assess how things are going. You need to act as a manager holding yourself to account, checking on progress and being honest with feedback.

How do you know if you're getting to where you want to unless you check-in with yourself and monitor progress, find solutions for issues and identify what may need to be modified to enable your success.

Hold a personal one-to-one. You can take it in turns to buy each other a coffee to mix it up a little if you like!

1.16 Monthly Performance Review

If you're having weekly one-to-ones why would you need a Monthly Performance Review?

Think of this as stepping back even further and reviewing where you are, where you're going and what you've achieved.

In section 5.3, Keeping Your Public Happy, we'll cover making your goals public to keep you motivated. Your monthly performance review is also your opportunity to update those around you on progress. Doing this every week is probably too often and the gains you achieve over seven days are probably not great enough to update on. But over a month the gains will be enough to show others your progress.

I'm not talking about graphs and spreadsheet reports. I am talking about being honest about what's happened and where you are against the plan.

Ask yourself:
"Does the plan need to change?"

"Does the amount of time you devote need to increase (or decrease)?"
"What if I did it slightly differently?"
"Who can help me drive things forward?"
"Who can I get to do this or that task for me?"

Being clear on a regular (and formal) basis with yourself and others will keep you on track better than if you just complete actions on your own.

What gets measured gets done. Measure it. Discuss it. Adapt it.

2 EFFICIENCY

"Efficiency is doing things right; effectiveness is doing the right things" - Peter Drucker

If it's all about focus and doing the right things, why is the second part of this book about efficiency?

In this technological world we use all sorts of programs on computers, Apps on smart phones, and websites on the Internet that take our valuable time. We have meetings and calls with people that take time. We have emails to wade through, calls on our time from other people needing a piece of us. There's the school run, or homework if you have kids. There are the chores that need doing which are boring but necessary.

We all have 86,400 seconds in each day. No more and no fewer (except when the clocks go back or forward or while travelling time zones of course, but usually). They're a precious resource that need to be managed to get as much out of them as possible.

Becoming more efficient at using the apps, websites, and programs that you need to use (Focus) will save you a heap of time. Cutting down meeting times, managing your calendar and touching stuff only once will free up more of those seconds for you to focus and take action towards your goals. And it will enable you to have time to be more connected to yourself, your family, and your friends.

I had a colleague whose work rate was double that of others in the same team simply because they had focused on getting super-efficient. I'll let you guess who got the promotion and achieved the most.

Drive for efficiency in everything you do. It'll make a huge difference.

2.1 Avoid Unnecessary Meetings

I came up with a new verb last week. It'll put you off your lunch.

It's about those regular meetings other people set up and invite you to. The project manager, on whatever the latest must do corporate topic is, sends out a series of 'check-ins' for you to attend at 5pm every day for 30 minutes. The boss diaries the weekly call with everyone on the team, plus the extended team members who support his team.

Jeez! Now you get invited to another team's weekly meetings so that you can spend an hour listening to what everyone else is doing while trying to complete your own tasks without being noticed at the back of the room (hello multi-tasking! Remember to bin the Swiss Army Knife). You speak for maybe 3 minutes of the hour, and only after you hear your name and realise you haven't a clue what the question was. Your 3 minutes of fame made no sense to anyone else either.

Your calendar is now full of regular meetings and calls that you want to get rid of as soon as possible. They leave you feeling in need of a dash to the toilet to purge yourself.

The new verb is 'To Diarrhoearise' meetings (as opposed to diarise them). A regular and never-ending stream of meetings and calls you could really do without. They are unwanted, leave you feeling washed out, are a pain in the backside, leave you sweating, and are a massive time-waster.

Meetings are, along with social media, the biggest time-wasters on the planet. You know that old slogan/joke that goes something like "If you're feeling bored or lonely at work just set up a meeting".

Work time is not social time. It may be that you can be social with work colleagues but during working hours we should all be working, and a meeting should be a work related activity that has a purpose and clear objectives with active participants.

Unless a meeting has a clear agenda, actually needs you there as an active participant, is relatively short, and has only a small number of people in it then decline the invitation.

There's a study that shows the larger a group of people the more complex and poor decisions are. And, the more collective time is wasted. Parkinson's Law (see section 5.2 for more on this) states that work expands to fill the time available, therefore if a meeting is scheduled for a long time, guess what? It'll take that length of time.

Only hold short, maximum 30 minute meetings and only with a maximum of 5-6 other people at a time.

Take the Imodium of the working world and decline meetings that aren't necessary, properly set up, or too long/big. You'll save yourself so much time.

2.2 Stand-up for Efficiency

When you are holding a meeting try mixing it up a little. It's harder to do this when you're the 'guest' at someone else's but when you're in control you can do what you like.

- Take the chairs away
- Ban laptops from the tables
- Put mobiles and tablets on silent, then in pockets or bags (face down on the table is ok too)

Hold your meeting standing up and get people to focus. You will be amazed at how quickly you can motor through the things that are important and make some real decisions together.

This approach stops people thinking a meeting is somewhere to set up their temporary office for an hour, working on their own stuff while sort of not quite listening and certainly not actively participating.

And, don't offer tea and coffee at the start of a meeting. It's not a social gathering. People can get a drink before and bring it with them if they want. The meeting is a massive use of resources and should be run as efficiently and effectively as possible. Think about the last few meetings you've been in and do the maths - the number of people multiplied by the average hourly rate multiplied by the duration of the meeting. Expensive.

To make your stand-up meetings work well you should nominate a chairperson and a scribe. Rotate them every meeting. It is the chairperson's job to move things through the agenda swiftly and efficiently. It is the scribe's job to write down what was agreed, who owns each item, and by when it's getting done.

Rotating the jobs is important so that everyone has to participate and is kept fresh. Everyone feels like they have some ownership of the meetings and the output.

Make your meetings stand-out by having them as stand-ups. Pretty soon everyone will love your meetings because they are short, punchy and get stuff accomplished.

2.3 To Do List App

You've written your project lists and your sub-lists. The goals, actions and sub-actions (process goals) have been defined and really thought about in detail. You know what steps you need to take to get to your ultimate goal.

You can write them on paper, in a journal, or keep them on your notes apps (OneNote, Evernote, or just Notes on iPhone). Wherever you put them, keep them all in the same place so you're not having to hunt for where you wrote your list for one of your projects.

My advice is to get yourself a To Do list App. Something that's designed to work as a To Do list which gives you the opportunity to add tasks and deadline dates.

Should you have a different To Do list for each project? There are different schools of thought on this one. Some say yes. Create a separate list for each one and manage through each list once you schedule time to focus on each. Others say you should only have one To Do list because then you are never having to prioritise each project, you are only prioritising the tasks that need to be ticked off.

I suggest if you're disciplined enough to schedule blocks of time for each of the projects you've created based on how important each one is to you then you can have multiple lists running. If you're not disciplined enough to schedule blocks of time, we need to work on that (see 2.10 and 2.13). Then you can just put everything into one To Do list.

The important thing is to have a single To Do list App and ensure that everything you identify that needs to get done is added to the list and worked through one by one.

If you're interested in combining your To Do list App with the Important/Urgent Matrix from section 1.6 you could download an App like 'Eisenhower' as this lets you put things in the categories of Do, Schedule, Delegate and Don't Do.

2.4 What's Your Password?

How many passwords do you have? If you're smart it will be the same number as the number of websites you have an account for. So how many websites and Apps have you ever signed up to? Hundreds I'll bet.

I am guessing but you probably don't have 100 unique passwords. You may have the really secure one for the important sites/Apps, and then a generic kind for everything else. Some of those will want you to have a special character as well as capitals and numbers, others won't let you. Then there are websites where you used to have a password you could remember but you forgot it and had to reset, forcing you to create another password that's probably just a variant of your normal one that you're bound to remember, only you can't when you next need it so you have to reset again.

"Aha! "You cry, "Google remembers my passwords and so do my smartphone apps." Indeed, but what when there's an app upgrade or you clear the cache on Chrome? Or when Google gets hacked?

I cannot remember all my passwords and I used to waste time trying to guess and then locking myself out, only to eventually have to reset and gain access 20 minutes after I wanted to use it. Such a waste of time and effort.

If you want to reclaim time, thereby improving your productivity, AND be so much more secure you should get a password manager.

There are plenty around but the one I recommend is LastPass (LastPass.com). It's free for 1 user or you can pay £2.33 per month for the ability to share between your devices and get back-up. For very little extra a month (£3.50 in total) you can get a family edition which allows you to have 6 family members use it with their own accounts.

LastPass has one super-password that's so super-impossible to crack and then it manages all passwords across sites for you. You don't have to remember any passwords ever again, except the super one.

This simple (and, for me, free) step has saved me so much time.

2.5 Templates for Anything

When you're given a blank sheet of paper and told to create something it's hard. You have to think what sections you want. What information you need to cover. What length each section should be. Once you have a structure you can then set about doing the work and creating the masterpiece.

When I write a song I know that it needs a verse, probably two, a chorus, a bridge/middle eight, a chorus, a verse and then another chorus. It'll usually have an intro and outro too. The words will typically rhyme at the end of each line. They will take the listener on a journey. The chorus is a bit more catchy.

Think about the pop industry. The songs are broadly the same in structure. Some break the mould (Bohemian Rhapsody) but by and large they are a kind of paint by numbers exercise.

Think about your favourite TV cop drama. Washed up, troubled, alcoholic cop called in to a murder scene. Bit of tension between them and another in the department. A clue takes them down a rabbit hole. It all seems so pointless as they can't break it. Then the genius, troubled, alcoholic cop spots something no-one else saw, and boom! The case gets solved super quick. Cut to alcoholic cop in bar brooding while he nurses another double.

I may be simplifying and exaggerating to make a point, but these shows are formulaic and that's why we like them. 24 season 2 is basically the same as 24 season 1. Every novel or film has a story arc with a few mini climaxes or terrible things that put the protagonists in jeopardy. And then there's a resolution.

It makes it easier to do things quickly if you have a template or formula.

If you're a blogger, set up a blogging template - 500 words total, intro, personal story or interesting fact, develop the theme, conclusion, ask readers for their thoughts. If you're training for a cycle ride create your template/formula for your warm-up or nutrition/hydration routine. If you're a writer, set up your template and then fill in the blanks.

I do not suggest this will make the quality any better than it would have been if you hadn't used a template, but it will make it quicker to get to your first draft and give you the all-important time needed to edit and refine for your second draft.

Where possible, in whatever you're trying to achieve, try to create templates so you can more speedily start and then complete the tasks you have on your list.

2.6 Two Screens

I work on my MacBook Pro 15". I take it everywhere. The battery lasts for ages and it is really fast to boot up. It's super easy to use and I love using it. Only, the screen is small, smaller than a single sheet of A4. That makes it easy to carry around but really hard to do serious work on.

I write books (like this one) and blog posts on Accelerate Performance (accelerate-performance.com), as well as work on spreadsheets, PowerPoint presentations and client proposals. For all of these I often need to refer to some research, or another document, or a website. On my 15" that means having to flick between screens multiple times while working, which is really quick and easy, but it interrupts the flow and makes everything take that little bit longer.

I also have a 27" iMac which has a super-large screen where I can easily have multiple documents open at the same time. With my MacBook open next to it I have two screens and ample ability to keep all the relevant information in view as I work.

Whether you're a Mac or PC user doesn't matter. You can easily set up a couple of screens with your laptop thereby giving yourself oodles of space for lots of relevant things (remember, we want to declutter - section 3.10 - so only have relevant stuff on show).

One added advantage of having two screens (or even just one big one) is that your working posture will be better. Looking down at a laptop screen isn't brilliant for your neck and shoulders whereas lifting your head to look straight ahead at two (or one) large screen is much kinder to you in the long run.

Do it for efficiency and for health reasons.

2.7 Don't Lose Your Mind

How long does the average piece of work take when you set your mind to it? Hard to quantify I know, as different tasks take different amounts of effort over different time periods. But let's say that it takes 2 hours to write a short article. That's the actual writing of the first draft. A load of research will have gone into it before that, but the actual writing of rough draft number one is 2 hours.

Then there's the editing for the second draft. Another hour perhaps. Lastly you add some images to it and it's good to go. Four hours in total. Not bad. Only you forgot to save it and the program crashed! Gone. Four hours of work down the drain.

This may sound like a statement of the bleeding obvious but you MUST remember to save your work. I've been in the working world for more years than I care to remember and only fairly recently have I lost something I'd worked on.

My website runs on WordPress and I set about updating the social settings, SEO title, keywords and a whole bunch of other things in the control panel and forgot to press 'Update'. I navigated away from the page by going into the visual editor and then headed back to the back-end to double check the settings I'd changed earlier. All gone!

Whatever you're doing, in whatever tool you're doing it in, keep saving your work. You never know when the gremlins will strike and your hard work evaporates. Sure, you can do it again but it's a real waste of time and it won't be as good second time round (it just never is, at least for me).

Don't lose your work and you won't need to lose your mind over it.

2.8 Shortcuts to Success

I have, on many occasions, collaborated with others putting together presentations for an event or two and, being a bit of a control freak, I prefer to drive the creation of the presentation deck. I'm pretty quick at it because I've used PowerPoint a lot. I'm not the quickest, and when there's someone else who is as speedy as the Roadrunner, I'll relinquish command and let them dazzle us.

When I've been a participant rather than the driver, and the person putting the deck together isn't a speed freak, I find it quite frustrating, because it's slower than it need be. I have no challenge with the content being created or how it looks. It's just slow. This section of the book is all about driving efficiency so that you have more hours available in the day for the important stuff so you need to focus on how to get more out of these programs.

Here's an example: There's a text box that needs duplicating so the driver of the PowerPoint highlights it, moves their cursor to the menu bar, clicks on Edit, moves the cursor down to Copy, clicks it, then moves the cursor back to Edit in the menu, navigates to Paste and finally moves the duplicated text box into position. It doesn't take more than about 10 seconds in total, but all these 10 seconds make up minutes that could have been spent getting on with the work. The speedy user will spend less than 2 seconds clicking Ctrl+C then Ctrl+V.

Every program has keyboard shortcuts. If you're going to be using something regularly then try to learn the shortcuts as they will save you loads of time, and in doing so won't break your concentration, enabling you to accomplish things a lot quicker.

True, it will take you time to learn them in the first place, but the investment is worth it. Soon enough the shortcuts become autopilots (habits) that you don't even have to think about.

2.9 Learn the Ropes

In a study at Standish Group in 2002 the chairman announced that 64% of features in software are not used. This has become the go-to metric. The world now seems to think that only 36% of software features are regularly used. But he was actually talking about four internally developed projects and not about software use as a whole.

So what's the real answer? Some people out there say 95% features aren't used. Others say it stands to reason that the 80:20 rule probably applies. No-one really seems to know for sure.

One thing is likely to be true though. You probably don't use all the clever stuff these programs have to offer. Microsoft Excel is an unbelievably complex and useful tool, as are the other Microsoft Office programs. There are Apps that do things you probably haven't learned about yet. Things in the settings that weren't immediately obvious but enable you to do cool stuff quickly.

I've been using an iPhone since they came out and am still learning how some things work. I discovered recently that holding down the space bar turns the keypad into a mousepad. Very useful indeed for getting the blinking cursor to go to precisely the right point in the text I'm editing.

I urge you to scratch the surface and really learn what the programs and Apps that you use can do so you get the most out of them. This will make life faster and your work more comprehensive.

Learn the ropes to get the most out of these amazing creations and use them to your advantage.

2.10 Control Your Schedule

In Section 2.1 we looked at the issue of people 'diarrhoearising' endless meetings that aren't well structured or planned, and why you should avoid pointless meetings. We looked at how to make them more efficient in 2.2 with a new stand-up meeting regime.

This section is about being in control of your whole calendar, and everything that goes in it.

Most calendar Apps enable others to see when you have an appointment, or even the precise detail of each event. You usually have to allow specific access for others to have full visibility, or you can make the calendar public.

There's a notion that in a collaborative team environment we must all share and be transparent with each other. We must be available and work in harmony. Enabling others to see your calendar is part of that open, trust environment that says we are one family, etcetera, etcetera....

Having your calendar visible to everyone is the best way to make sure people can legitimately fill it up with their stuff and say, "It showed you had a gap between meetings so I blocked your calendar then". Great!! Just because you don't have a specific meeting with someone does not mean you have nothing to do. You need space to actually do some work!

A close friend has had a couple of bosses who told him that he needed to make his calendar open to them and the rest of the team. There was no company policy that said he had to. He refused to do it on the grounds that his agenda was his business to manage in order that he efficiently drives to achieve the goals the business has set him. It was suggested he may not want to open it up because he had something to hide! He countered that the only reason this would be requested is if there was a lack of trust! Eventually he decided he didn't want to work for a boss like that. I have sympathy with his approach. In all the teams I have ever managed I have NEVER asked or told them to make their calendar public to me. Some have done so because that was their choice but others never have and I have NEVER asked anyone to. I don't need to delve into their calendars to know where they are or what they're up to. I know this because I work closely with them on a daily basis.

It is about controlling your agenda based on the tasks you have to complete. It's about scheduling in the time to complete these. That is like scheduling a meeting with yourself to undertake a piece of work that is on your important list.

Don't get me wrong, I'm not suggesting you can't be flexible and move stuff around when an important meeting needs to take precedence, or a team member needs some coaching, or your loved one needs to speak to you, but I am advocating taking control of your calendar and managing it to suit the things you want or need to achieve, be they work or personal objectives.

After all, you are an adult and should be trusted to manage your time appropriately to get done what needs to get done.

2.11 It's Mail Time

It's like a badge of honour in offices all over the world.

"I got 200 emails yesterday'. "That's nothing, I had 300!" Or whatever the number is. Maybe it makes people feel needed. Maybe it's just a bit of harmless bragging.

Whatever it is, and however many you get a day, it's important to be super-efficient with how you manage them.

If you're getting a lot of emails every day they will be filling your inbox up at a fair old rate, like a bath filling with water. You could stand there with a little beach bucket while you're also trying to do something that requires attention and effort like, for example, learn a foreign language while trying to intercept the water flowing into your bath, one bucket at a time. You then tip that bucket of water down the hand basin and go back to do it again while trying to concentrate on learning "Dónde está la farmacia¿".

Or you could focus on learning the key Spanish phrases uninterrupted so you can find the pharmacy with that monster hangover while on holiday, and then, when you've finished that task, pull the plug out of the bath tub once you have some time to dedicate to the task of bath emptying.

It is so much more efficient to keep your emails together and schedule specific times of day to deal with them. You avoid the constant interruption and concentration switching costs of dealing with the constant stream. Schedule to deal with emails mid-morning, after you've completed the three most important tasks of the day (1.3). Then schedule again mid-afternoon, and lastly right before you switch off for the day.

If you schedule your emails and manage them in blocks you'll be able to concentrate much better on the tasks that really matter, uninterrupted, and it will take up considerably less of your day than if you allowed yourself to give in to the constant, needy stream of stuff filling your inbox.

2.12 One Touch to Zero

Still on the topic of emails, get into the habit of breaking them down into different groups.

1. Require personal action
2. Delegate
3. For info only, and then delete

Those that need personal attention should be done straight away (see section 4.5 for more) or scheduled, actually put into your To Do list and your calendar (that you're now in control of thanks to 2.10).

Those that can be delegated should be sent to the new owner with a clear message about what you expect and by when. Then set up an automated reminder for both you and the new owner so it pops up and reminds you both that it's due. If the new owner hasn't done it chase them but be clear it is their responsibility to complete the task.

If something's been sent for info, read it and bin it. You may feel you want to keep it for reference later, and that's fine, but many of these types of emails go out of date quickly, so speak to the project owner when you need the most up to date view.

At the end of the working day your aim is to have nothing unread in your email inbox. It should all have been scheduled, delegated or binned, and anything you're keeping archived in a relevant folder.

Touch things once only and reduce your inbox to zero every single day. Take control of your schedule and manage the important tasks to completion while ensuring that those which can be delegated are being managed by others.

2.13 Group Stuff Like a Pro

In this book we touch on the switching cost of moving from one task to another and never really concentrating uninterrupted on the important tasks. Every time you allow yourself to be distracted you defocus, losing the thread of where you've been. It may seem that a quick and easy little task doesn't take much thought so doesn't really distract, but even an easy distraction takes your mind away from what you were engaged in.

Say you're trying to write a part of your dissertation paper and are looking at some complex data that needs analysis. A quick thing then comes in that you can easily just say yes to via email, so you do. You try to get back to where your mind was with the complex data and at best it'll take you a good few minutes to refocus and at worst it'll take a lot longer.

Don't give in to those distractions.

One way to ensure you stay distraction free is to group your tasks together into similar types of activity. Schedule your email time (2.11). Focus on social media for 15 minutes a day at a specific time (see section 3.6). Whatever groupings your tasks can be put into batch the similar types of tasks together.

Here's a ridiculous example to illustrate the point. You are training for a triathlon and are in the process of writing a book. Which of these two scenarios sounds best to you?

> 1. You start writing the next chapter, then you do your swimming warm up in the pool (careful not to splash your PC). Next you do some research for your book (careful not to get the pages wet). Then onto the bike for a 10k cycle. Now the library to check on a specific journal, followed by a run home, a quick review of the first draft of the book and, finally, a shower.

> 2. Go to the Library to review the journal, research the book and finally begin the chapter. Next review the draft. On to the bike to the swimming pool, a few laps front crawl and backstroke, a quick ride home and then a short run, all topped off with a nice relaxing shower.

It's obvious, and yes it's a silly example, but it illustrates the point. If you batch tasks together which are similar in nature it'll make you a whole heap more efficient. Get into the habit of grouping stuff like a pro.

3 DISTRACTION

Ping. Beep. Notification. Social Media. Call. Text. Chat. Ping. Beep. Notification…….

Getting down to the tasks you need to complete can feel like hard work. It is important work (as it's focused on your goals now) and the more you put into it the better you'll do and the quicker it'll be done.

But isn't it nice to break the work up with some interesting or fun things? It makes the day seem more engaging and keeps you feeling connected to others as well as the outside world.

And yet - no! You may feel all those things but if you're interested in getting things done you need to eliminate, or if that's not possible, minimise the Distractions that take you away from being focused.

According to McKinsey, 28% of working hours are spent dealing with email and messages. They estimate that social media costs the US economy $650 billion every year in lost productivity. We are all addicted to being connected today in a way that didn't exist 30 years ago before the invention of the internet. Further research conducted in the US found that typical workers are distracted every 11 minutes and can take up to 25 minutes to settle back down to the task that was interrupted.

Carnegie Mellon University conducted a study where people were asked to read a passage and answer questions. Those who were interrupted during the process scored only 80% of those who were uninterrupted.

3.1 No, No, Notifications

How many Apps do you have on your phone and computer combined? 100? More? Probably most of these don't get used that often. There will be a few work-horses that are your go-to Apps for working, browsing and playing. All of them are vying for your attention.

Check your Notification settings and count the number which are set to off. By default, they are on, so you'd have to have gone in and turned them off yourself if they are off. Then have a look at those that are on and see that they can notify you through Banners, Sounds and Badges. That's three ways they will shout at you and distract.

Maybe it's something spooky about my phone in particular but I swear I didn't make any changes to any Notifications recently and yet I started getting messages ping up from Twitter telling me that 'So and So' has tweeted. Maybe the App updated and defaulted back to standard. Maybe it was user error. Maybe my phone has a ghost.

The Notification dropdown on my Mac is permanently set to Do Not Disturb. I just checked and had it not been I'd have had about a dozen interruptions in the past 30 minutes alone.

All these Notifications are trying really hard to distract from your chosen tasks. They are probably jealous you're heading towards achieving something wonderful!

Do yourself a favour and turn ALL your Notifications OFF. You will already be getting used to scheduling activity such as checking messages and emails, as well as the tasks on your To Do lists. If you need to check on a specific App then schedule that too.

Stop them from distracting you. Every distraction is costing you time and concentration. You can read more about the elimination of these types of distraction in section 3.8 DND. Always DND.

3.2 Apps and Websites

My To Do list still has lots on it but I'll just check the cricket score quickly before I carry on. Australia 143 all out! What a monster performance by the England bowlers. Let me quickly check out Jimmy Anderson's bowling stats. What a legend. Go Jimmy!

Now the weather. What's the weather going to be like tomorrow for Day Three of the Test Match at Lord's? Mostly cloudy, possible light rain later. That'll mean a bit of fun for the Aussie bowlers later on.

I'm just going to check what Aggers is saying on TMS through the BBC website. Yep. He also thinks it's not going to be easy for England in the middle tomorrow but he's saying Joe Root should have no trouble against the Australian spin.

Quick check of the email App. Nothing interesting there. Now how's the Chaise Longue getting on on eBay? Oh, 4 watchers. Interesting.

Ok. Wow. I've only got 20 mins left to complete the next two tasks......

Stop with all the Apps and websites! They don't need you and you don't need them while you're working. It is so

easy to get distracted by other stuff that seems more interesting, and as the above scenario shows it's really very easy to move from one App to another for 'just a minute'. Those 'just a minutes' add up and waste time.
No problem to check those apps and websites at some point during the day, but save them until your down-time, after you've done what you set out to do.

If you really struggle with this discipline go to section 3.11 for some useful Apps (ironically) that will seriously help.

3.3 Dump the Subscriptions

Over time we sign up to all sorts of newsletters, updates from websites, new voucher codes, and the like. We follow people and businesses on social media. At the time of signing up and following they were no doubt of interest. The question is, are they still relevant and aligned with your current lifestyle and plans?

When I was into running, on my middle-aged quest to prove I was still young, I signed up to a number of websites and blogs that provided me with training tips and discounts to gels and protein shakes to aid recovery. They were extremely useful, and I achieved my goal.

These days I run a bit but only because I feel I need to stay fit(ish). I'm no longer interested in buying pills to help my VO2 Max increase, or Creatin supplements. And if I never enter a race again it will be too soon.

Rather than keep my inbox clogging up with these emails, which take time to scan and/or delete, I unsubscribed. I put all emails of this type into a folder over the course of a week and then spent a happy half hour unsubscribing. I did the same with people I'm connected to or follow on social media. If I didn't unfriend them I did at least unfollow some.

I'm not advocating unsubscribing or unfollowing everything. Just those things that you don't need anymore. Here's a quick tip: If you have a Gmail email address (or a service that has Gmail underneath) you can subscribe to websites using an augmented email address so that the subscriptions get tagged. For example if your email is yourname@gmail.com you could subscribe to 'Pheasant Fanciers Weekly' using the email yourname+pheasant@gmail.com and it will be received by you as normal. For 'Craft Brewing Boors Monthly' it's yourname+boors@gmail.com. The thing you do is add '+whatever' between your name and @gmail.com.

Then you can set up a rule in your email that automatically adds emails received by each bespoke address to a specific folder so you have them all neatly together and so you can batch your reading for when you have time.

(Unfortunately, I don't know if this does or doesn't work for other email providers. I would be interested to find out. Email me and let me know.)

3.4 News is So Yesterday

The news is so depressing. It's full of war, death, disease, fighting (politicians and others). And while it may be new today it's old before you can say "What happened?"

I know people who pour over all the articles and opinion pieces, who are constantly listening to the radio or watching News 24, or something similar. And that is OK if you're a journalist, politician, or political/current affairs commentator. It's also OK if you choose to do that and don't have other things to do where you need to reclaim some time.

But if you have something you want to get done then go on a news diet.

I don't suggest a complete black-out because it's a good thing to know what's happening out there. You would make yourself a tedious dinner guest if you knew nothing about current affairs and you'd find it difficult to hold your own in a conversation. Some things are important and worth knowing. The whole #MeToo movement in 2018 was really important. Knowing the potential impact to us in Britain as a result of Brexit is important - it's the biggest thing to happen to the country since the Second World War. But a lot of the news is a time-waster.

Pick a good news summary App or feed and get the main points from reading the potted versions. You can keep up to date without spending a lot of time on it.

3.5 Check Your Phone Last

It's so tempting to roll over, groggy eyed and reach for the phone as soon as you wake. So many people now use their phone as an alarm clock that it's almost inevitable it becomes the first thing that's touched in the morning.

I read somewhere that iPhones (and presumably other smart phones) are used more for telling the time than anything else. Who knows if that's just benign fake news or it's true but it wouldn't surprise me. I don't wear a watch and tap the screen to find out what the time is.

It's quite hard to avoid your phone first thing in the morning. The news, Facebook, and emails are all waiting for you, calling for you to look at them (they are so needy!).

My tip for avoiding distractions and improving your productivity so that you accelerate towards your north star is to check your phone last, after you've done other more important things.

Get up, exercise, shower, eat something, do the first couple of tasks you set out the night before. Then you can check your phone. It'll still be there and by the time you've seen that the politicians are still arguing, or Jo's cat brought up a mammoth fur ball at 11.27 last night you will have broken the back of other really important tasks.

In the first hour of the day do not check your phone. Get on with something useful. You can even make checking your phone a reward for having achieved something marvellous (see section 5.4).

3.6 It's SoMe Time

Social Media is a big part of life. It can be brilliant. I have learned stuff from tweets and updates that friends, companies and public figures have posted. I use it to promote my work and company. I use it to update friends on my music projects. It has, or can have, some really good benefits.

But it can be the biggest waste of time known to woman, man and beast. Trawling through endless posts and updates on the best meal ever, the boring commute, the picture of a horse, cats (cat pictures!), dogs, when it snows, the latest half-formed opinions of social influencers who are paid to promote whatever they spout forth about, political opinion, fake news, Brexit, Trump, cosmetics, Jenner and that Kardashian lot.

Scroll. Like. Like. Scroll. Scroll. Read. Like. Scroll. Troll. Scroll. Like, Troll. Etc.. Ad nauseam.

Don't get me wrong, I'm not a complete dinosaur. I can see the fun in it and the uses. But it is, for many people, out of control, especially if their aim is to do something amazing to get more productive and reach the stars.

Make Social Media time "So Me" time. The time of day it's always "Me time". Alone for a few minutes doing nothing in particular but one where you're seated and comfortable. That's right, on the loo. I don't know about you but I feel this sort of thing can't be rushed. Think of Noel Coward's character Mr Bridger from 'The Italian Job'. He was most upset to have been disturbed while reading on the toilet.

Make time for social media but limit it to 15 minutes a day and multi-task while you do it, on the loo. It's the one time I approve of multi-tasking.

3.7 Once an Hour Only

How often do you check your phone? A survey of 2,000 Americans showed that on average people check their phones every 12 minutes, which is 5 times per hour. In a 16 hour day this equates to 80 times a day. That's 80 distractions a day.

1 in 10 admitted to checking their phone every 4 minutes. That's 240 times a waking day! Serious problem territory there.

How long do you think each phone check takes? A couple of seconds? Minutes? You can do the maths. It's a lot of time on nothing much at all.

62% of respondents said they'd rather go without chocolate for a week than their phones. 60% reported occasional stress when the phone was off or out of reach. 31% feel regular anxiety when it's not available. A staggering 40% said they'd rather lose their voice for a day than be without their phone for the same period.

This is a major addiction. One that is now well understood, with Apple and others making strides to help people use their devices less. I now get regular updates on how much screen time I've used each week (mostly used on Goole Maps I reckon…..how did we ever survive before Google Maps? I'd be lost without it! Haha!)

If you want to reclaim time for your projects and goals then implement a rule that says you will check your phone a maximum of once per hour. Fewer times than that is fine. But make it no more than once.

3.8 DND. Always DND

Sadly in today's 'always connected' world people are often pretty rude to each other. The phone sits on the table in front of them and when it pings they glance at it, pick it up, and deal with the message straight away while the other person is sat waiting.

If you were a doctor or therapist you'd focus 100% on your patient/client during their appointment. You simply can't use your mobile at all. If you schedule a meeting with your boss you would likely focus on them and the agenda items to the exclusion of everything else. It's unlikely you'll be getting the big bonus or raise if your boss thinks you don't care enough about the meeting by answering other calls or messages while giving them an update on an important client.

The main thing here is that you can choose to avoid being disturbed when it's important enough or when using your phone is simply not allowed (during a concert, on a flight).

Choose to be undisturbed when you are focusing on your goals and being ultra-productive. Put yourself into DND mode - 'Do Not Disturb'.

Turn notifications off on your phone and computer. Put Do Not Disturb on your phone. If you really want you can put yourself on airplane mode to ensure you can't be contacted. Disconnect from the internet if that helps.
My recommendation is to turn notifications off and put DND on.

This will stop all distractions however, including those from important people you may actually want or need to hear from. Do you really want to block your child from calling in an emergency, or your boss or spouse? My further recommendation is to create a list of Favourites on your phone who will still get through to you with a call if they really need to contact you while you're on DND.

Steps:
- Turn notifications off
- Put all devices on DND
- Create a list of important callers who you are happy to be disturbed by
- Tell those in your list that to get hold of you they MUST call and not just text or email

3.9 Messages Will Derail

I use a Mac, a PC, an iPhone, and an iPad. All have instant messenger and email on them. And no matter what device I'm working on I'm constantly interrupted by messages heralding themselves as they arrive, shouting "read me now!" I tell you it takes a lot of will power not to casually glance to see what it's about….after all, who knows if it's important, or more interesting?!

If something is really important to the sender they can call you, and if the person who's calling you is important then there's a way to make sure you can be reached as we've looked at in the previous section, 3.8.

Emails and messages are not important enough to interrupt your work. We've looked at batching tasks together and scheduling your workload, including dealing with emails in sections 2.10 and 2.13.

Let's get rid of the distractions.

- If you run Gmail through Chrome there's an extension called 'Inbox When Ready' that will hide your Inbox for a defined period of time
- Turn off the sound notifications alerting when a message has arrived
- Mute notifications on WhatsApp and other messaging apps
- Hide your email inbox by removing it from the app bar, or putting it in a group on the iPhone that's with other message apps on the second page
- Stop the email preview notifications in Mail, Outlook or whatever program you use for your emails - just how distracting is that little box that tells you the subject of a new email?

Find all the message related distractions and eliminate them. Then take control of your time and schedule specific sessions during the day when YOU want to deal with them (remember to touch them only once and either Do, Schedule, or Delegate).

3.10 Clutter Free Desktop

You boot up and see a mass of files greeting you from the desktop. What's where? It's a mess. And then when you want to find something you have to scan your eyes over everything to see where it is. Big time waster.

Create a folder system and subdivide into further folders relating to different groups of topics. Then file stuff, and make a habit of it. It'll be like a spring clean for your computer and it'll help declutter your brain.

Why is this important? Because if you're working in a cluttered environment then your brain won't be quite as focused and 'in the zone' as you need it to be.

While you're working away on a document make sure it is full screen size so that you can literally see nothing other than what you're working on. On a Mac you can make it really full screen so it removes the header and applications bars (you can also set the Mac up to automatically hide the applications bar in Settings).

When browsing the internet try using an extension like Clearly from Evernote. It will present you with a distraction free view of the content alone so you can focus on the messages and not on flashing adverts or offers or anything else (oh, look a rabbit....!). There are plenty of other alternatives available but I'm a prolific user of Evernote as my go to tool for clipping websites and writing notes so Clearly is easy for me to use.

Find something that works for you and then get your desktop clutter free so you can focus solely on the tasks at hand.

3.11 Block and Tackle

If you really don't have the discipline to stop yourself from casually browsing apps and websites when you have important work to do then there are some useful tools that'll keep you focused.

This list is not exhaustive and is likely to change over time as new tools become available, but for now, dive in to one of them and stop the distraction of other stuff while you're on your path to achievement and glory.

1. Freedom - https://freedom.to - This is a paid for app you download to iOS, Android, Mac or Windows. Once you have it you can run it on multiple devices. There's also an extension for Chrome, Firefox and Opera. There's a free trial version that lets you block a small number of things but the paid version (Premium) is pretty cost effective with an option to pay monthly, annually (significant discount) or lifetime (super significant discount). At the time of writing they were also offering a 30% discount with a pop-up that only appears when you're quite the way down

the page or look like you're about the exit the page. Freedom can block specific sites, the whole internet, and/or apps. It can be set up on a schedule and will sync between your different devices.

2. StayFocusd - Here we have one of the many browser extension offerings. It is only available as a Chrome extension and is free. You can search for it by browsing extensions in Chrome. It enables you to set time limits so you can still browse at certain points once the time limits have elapsed. The drawback is that it only sits on your device with Chrome and so there's nothing stopping a determined time-waster from grabbing their phone to check Facebook, or whatever.

There are plenty of other extensions available for various browsers, though they tend to be biased towards either Chrome or Mac/iOS.

If you're struggling to stay away from the apps and websites and need a blocker then I highly recommend you go for something like Freedom and pay the money. It's an investment in you and your goal achievement.

And perhaps, if you're like me, you'll think "I'm going to use it even if I don't like the restrictions it imposes because I paid for it and want to get the maximum benefit from something that cost me money!"

4 ACTION

In Section 1, Focus, we looked at how the 181 mile journey that Google Maps told you would take 2h43m will take an infinite amount of time if you don't actually start the car and start driving.

Without action there is inaction, and no-one ever achieved much by sitting around doing nothing.

Bill Gates took action. Steve Jobs took action. Usain Bolt took action. Mother Theresa took action. Sir Steve Redgrave, Sir Ben Ainslie, Dame Ellen MacArthur all took action. Debra Searle MBE MVO took action to complete her solo row across the Atlantic.

Anyone who you've ever heard of who achieved something, took action. Those who focused and channelled their action towards their goals achieved something, even if it wasn't quite what they'd initially planned.

Learn to take action and drive towards your goals. If it turns out you're not going in quite the right direction, then take action to change course.

The key is to DO. Always Be Doing. ABD.

In this section of the book we'll look at how perfection is an illusion, that the start is the most important thing, where to start, what to do first and second, and putting in place a 30 day plan.

4.1 This Harmful Illusion

We all love an illusion. I remember being captivated by Paul Daniels, the late, great, and popular British magician. He was amazing. Real magic (to a child at least). Then there was David Copperfield, the illusionist on a grand scale. There have been plenty since, all of them captivating the audience with a collective gasp or 'What? How did they do that?"

Back down in the real world where Magic is just a radio station there's one illusion that's the enemy of the would-be achiever.

Perfection.

Perfection does not exist. It is the ultimate illusion. What's perfect to me is probably not to you, and vice versa. And to be honest, nothing is perfect for me really. It can always be improved upon somehow. The songs I recorded last Autumn are really good but every time I listen to them I think "Oh - I could have been a little better in tune on that note", and "I should have had some strings filling in there", and "That lyric could have been better." Most people won't notice the imperfections. But I do.

So, I could tinker with them and improve a bit, but is the improvement big enough to really warrant the effort? No. What if I said I can't move on to the next task on my To Do list until this one is perfect? I'd never get anything done.

Good, in the context of completing your process tasks towards your goal, is good enough. Obviously try to make everything you do as good as possible but don't let yourself fall into the trap of using "It's not perfect" as your chief procrastination tool and get out of jail free card.

One of the greatest lines in a song is from 'All of Me' by John Legend;

"Love your curves and all your edges,
All your perfect imperfections."

Not only is he spot on that it is precisely because of imperfections that something can be perfect, but it's also an utterly imperfect rhyme, thereby proving the point very nicely.

4.2 Small or Tough?

Here is the age-old time management dilemma. Which way round do you start?

Do you start with the smallest and easiest tasks, thereby giving yourself the lift when you see how many you've quickly completed?

Or do you start with the hardest on the basis it will take the most effort and you should tackle it while you are freshest, then move on to the easier ones once you've got that brute under your belt?

Starting Small

The theory goes that if you start small or simple and move on to the next simplest then every task you ever do is the easiest of the ones you have left to complete. It's sound logic. Keep doing the easy stuff and then it's all easy.

Personally, I don't like this approach because I know in my heart of hearts I'm kidding myself. I know I'm only playing at the edges and the meatier items are just lurking, waiting to pounce.

It's like being on a gentle upward slope that gets a little steeper every time you take a step forward. Yes, the next step you take is going to be easier than the one after it but by the time you get to the end you have to jump up a vertical cliff edge.

Starting Tough

This is the macho approach. Find the toughest, psych yourself up for it and then 'bang', off you go. It's like doing a Tough Mudder race, then a half marathon, followed by a 10K run, then a 5K, and finally a stroll with the dog through the woods.

Each one gets easier and the sense of achievement when the tougher ones have been finished is really worthwhile.

Just make sure that if you choose this approach you also implement the other concepts in this book so you really focus, give yourself the right breathing space and reward yourself.

My advice is to focus on the important tasks whether they are small or tough and crack on (see section 4.3).

4.3 Just Start. Anywhere.

However you like to start (tough or small) there is one fundamental thing to remember. You actually need to start. Just start.

You've spent time building your project lists. You've defined your ultimate goals and added well thought through process goals along the way. The lists look endless. You might even feel a bit overwhelmed by it all.

You're not alone. I am an avid list writer and have plenty of goals. I get overwhelmed, often. Staring at your lists you may wonder where to start. This project or that? Which of the tasks to start with? Small or tough?

There are two steps:

1. Prioritise which project you'll tackle first
2. Then start something. IT DOESN'T MATTER WHAT OR WHERE

Seriously, it doesn't matter whether you start in the middle, towards the end or at the beginning. What matters is that you start. Start something that begins the journey towards your goal.

When a car starts moving it has to overcome the inertia of its own weight, along with friction of moving parts and the wind. It takes quite a bit to get over this initial inertia. But by the time the car is running along the road it takes less effort to keep it going. The momentum carries you down the road and it's quicker and less difficult to keep on moving.

It's the same for your projects. The first few steps are often daunting and tough, but once you're moving, momentum keeps you going.

It doesn't matter where you start. It just matters that you do start.

4.4 First, the Must Dos

In 4.2 we looked at whether to start small or start tough. There's no right answer. We're each likely to have a personal preference.

However, I would always advocate starting with the Must Dos.

Take the list from your important/urgent matrix or ABCDE and tackle the things that you must do ahead of anything else. These are likely to be the urgent ones if you're at the start of your achieving journey. Once you've been doing it a while you'll reduce the number of urgent things and have learned to delegate some of them.

If you've gone through the full process of defining your goals and the steps which need to be taken to get there in real detail, you'll know what the Must Dos are.

I would advocate doing these whether they are hard or easy. If they are important to your end result you should get on with them.

And remember, just start the first one and use the momentum that builds to keep ploughing through.

4.5 Next, the Quick Dos

Throughout every day there are new tasks which pop up. Ones you didn't see coming but nevertheless need to get done at some point.

Do they all need to go on your To Do list? Should you run all of them through your Important/Urgent qualification process? The answer is that it depends on how big the task is and how long it will take.

If it's the need to fill in a form for your team quiz night stating your team name, how many bottles of white/red/water you'll need to pre-order, and adding your credit card details for the entry fee, it's a task for the To Do list because that's going to take a bit of time and coordination with your team mates.

If it's that you discover you've pretty much run out of medication and need a repeat prescription and it takes approximately 90-120 seconds to log on to the doctor's website to request it or call their reception desk to ask, then just do it. Straight away.

Any tasks that pass the 'fewer than 2 minute' rule should get done immediately.

If they'll take longer, add them to your To Do list.

4.6 Schedule or Do. There is No Leave

When tasks that need to get done hit you there are three categories they should be put into:

1. **Do** - If it can be done in 2 minutes or fewer then do it.
2. **Schedule** - If it will take more that 2 minutes add it to your To Do list and schedule it.
3. **Delegate** - Do you need to do it or can someone else?

The key message is to schedule things that are on your To Do list. Actually create a diary entry with an allocated amount of time to get the actions done. Don't make the duration too long though. Keep it snappy (see section 5.2 for more).

Actually manage your schedule and slot your tasks in. Some are work, important work, and deserve dedicated time put in. Others are quick actions. Some don't need you at all because someone else is well placed to do them instead.

What you should never do is leave something thinking you'll come back to look at it later. Chances are you won't. You need never forget anything again simply by writing stuff down and scheduling it.

4.7 Actually Do These For 30 Days

Here's the challenge to you. Don't just read this book, nod and think "Yes, some of that sounds quite sensible. I'll try to get to some of these sometime." That'll get you nowhere.

My challenge to you is to do or schedule the use of a few (or more) of these tips right now.

Put your cup of coffee down and get that pad and pen out to write everything down. Write your lists and prioritise them. List all the distractions you suffer from on a daily basis and think about the quick wins that you can easily eliminate. Write your goals down and make them SMART. Schedule a one-to-one with yourself at the end of the week, and put a monthly recurring appointment in your calendar for a monthly performance review. Call your friend and tell them about the new you and what you're planning, no, GOING to do.

Do some of these for 30 days consistently. And make them part of your normal routine. In no time at all you'll do many of them out of force of habit.

But you need to start. Just start. With any of the 67 tips. It really doesn't matter where.

(The observant amongst you will notice this call to action in the middle of the book, before we've looked at the rest of the tips. That's because this is an action which fits into the action section.)

5 MOTIVATION

"Doing doesn't come from motivation; Motivation comes from doing."

So said a colleague of mine about twenty-five years ago. I had been complaining that I just didn't feel really motivated to do something. I think I may have said I "couldn't be arsed". That, despite the fact that it was something that I thought I wanted to do.

I suppose I believed that once I felt motivated, I'd suddenly get a spurt of energy and then everything would happen, I could sit back and feel super proud of myself for achieving it.

Only, if I ever got around to it, I'd probably complete it at some undefined time in the future. Maybe.

Something about his words struck a chord. If I just took one action, then I'd set up a chain of events that would have to follow. So, I did. A week later I was knee-deep in actions and deadlines and I achieved my goal. It was lots of work but the one thing I wasn't lacking throughout it all was motivation.

We all have different reasons for wanting to achieve something. We all have different motivators. It's really important to define your own purpose and know the Why? of what you're doing.

If you can anchor what you're doing with a strong Why?, then you'll be able to keep that as a guiding light to drive during the harder times.

Why do you want to achieve your goal? What's the reward? What's the meaning?

Then get on with it and keep the motivation pendulum swinging.

5.1 Play the Movie

What does it feel like to have achieved something great? Do you feel happy? Excited? Satisfied? Maybe it's all of those.

What do you imagine you'll see and hear? Are there people around you? Are you surrounded by noise? Or sitting, sipping a chilled glass of white on a veranda overlooking the sea?

What will you have as a result of your accomplishment? Will it result in a medal around your neck? Or a physical book on a shelf? Will it be a new car? Or perhaps the degree certificate hanging on the wall?

Whatever is important to you, write it down. Make a list of all the benefits you'll receive as a result of doing what you've set yourself. Break that list into the categories of Be, Do and Have. What will you Be? What will you Do? What will you Have? And list down the internal and external feelings and stimuli that will come your way.

Once you have the lists create a short movie in your mind. Visualise the sounds, people around you, and the location. Feel who you will become as a result. Add a plot line to the movie that shows what you're going to do, both as a result of simply achieving your goal and as a reward for success. Add another plot line that has you using the things you'll have once you're done.

Make the movie and play it in your head. Play it when things get tough and you feel your motivation waning. Play it when you feel excited, as a boost to your creativity and energy. Play it as part of the routine to keep you focused and motivated to complete the goals you've set.

As I trained and prepared to run the London Marathon, I visualised coming around the corner into The Mall towards the finish line. I'd seen it a hundred times on TV and thought how I'd feel and what I'd see. I imagined what I'd feel like afterwards. I saw the faces of children I'd be helping with the money raised for the NSPCC. Admittedly I actually felt exhausted, in pain, and like I couldn't stand up at the end. But I also did feel the sense of elation at completing something I never imagined would be possible for an asthmatic, middle-aged, giraffe.

These movies helped me during the dark and freezing-cold winter mornings at 5am while training. Without the movie playing in my head at those times I might not have stuck at it.

Become both a movie maker and movie star today by creating your own.

5.2 Under Pressure

I bet you can't read or say the words 'Under Pressure' without the bass riff of the Queen song rattling through your brain. It's iconic. Just like 'Can't Stop Me Now' and 'We Are The Champions'. Put them in that order for maximum impact. Build up some momentum with the first, keep on motoring with energy in the second and then achieve your goals and be your own champion. Simple.

You may wonder why being 'Under Pressure' is a good thing. Surely pressure is an enemy.

Nope. Pressure is your friend. Imagine you have all the time in the world to complete something. No pressure. No deadline. You do a load of other things as well (multi-tasking) and get distracted. Eventually you finish it but by then may have forgotten what it's part of or why you ever wanted to get it done.

Then imagine the same task has a deadline. This deadline is a couple of weeks away so you think "no need to jump on it now…. plenty of time". You leave it to the last minute and hit the deadline, but the bulk of the work was done in the last 24 hours. Phew, job done!

If you'd given yourself only 24 hours to do it in the first place it would have taken the same amount of effort, but you'd have completed it 13 days early. That sounds like a pretty good outcome. Move on to the next task and complete that. And the next…

Cyril Nothcote Parkinson wrote a piece in The Economist in 1955 about his observations from working in the British Civil Service. He stated that "Work expands so as to fill the time available for its completion". This has been coined as 'Parkinson's Law'.

The corollary to this is "If you wait until the last minute it only takes a minute to do." Or "Work contracts to fit the time we give it."

Set yourself deadlines for every task and make them short. This act alone will keep you motivated to crack on with completing the task. And the more you complete, the faster you get towards achieving your ultimate goal, thus providing even greater motivation to keep on going.

Remember, pressure is your friend. Put yourself under it. Play the Queen song as your constant reminder to adopt Parkinson's Law and squeeze the available time into a shorter duration.

5.3 Keeping Your Public Happy

If you keep your aspirations and goals to yourself, you're going to need to be super disciplined to run your own one-to-ones and monthly reviews. Perhaps the manager part of you will think it's ok to let things slide as you know how hard the worker part of you has been pushing and how tired they are.

If you only talk about things with yourself then how are you going to get the coaching, guidance and moral support that we all need from time to time?

Your Public could be your spouse or best friend, mum or dad, or work colleague. It could be all of them. It's your choice. But make them Your Public.

Why? Because they care about you and probably want to help. If you can clearly articulate why you're driving to achieve something they can buy into your journey and support you along the way. It's highly likely that whatever you're looking to do is going to take time away from them or the things you have done before, and so you really ought to share with them so they can support and understand the purpose.

They can guide you, help you, give you the talking to you may need, be a listening ear, and even take you away from the pursuit of performance when needed.

But there's another deeper psychological reason to consider doing this too.

We have a natural and subconscious desire to be congruent with commitments we make. Most people feel they are letting themselves and others down if they give up or don't complete something they committed to by a stated date. It's natural and inbuilt.

Why not use this to your advantage and commit what you're doing, and by when you intend to have it done, to Your Public? They will keep you honest and driving yourself so you don't let anyone, including them, down.

5.4 Mmmmmm....That Feels Good!

If you work and never rest we know the quality and quantity of the output diminishes (section 1.4 How to Concentrate Better). Even if you do rest you may feel a bit dull. Yes, you can see the green cells on the spreadsheet that show things are getting ticked off the action list. That makes you feel good but it's sometimes not inspiring enough on its own to keep you going at it.

Give yourself a reward every now and then. Set up a system whereby when you've achieved the first three or four items (or whatever works for you) on the action list you reward yourself with something. Then after completing the next few reward yourself again.

I'm not necessarily advocating spending lots of money on treats, or unhealthy biscuits, cakes or sweets. I mean having that cup of real coffee from the canteen upstairs and not the instant in the little kitchen area. Or giving yourself 15 minutes to browse your next holiday destination. Perhaps even book that holiday once you've achieved the main goal.

Whatever you consider a treat, schedule it in and work towards it. Give yourself a reward for achievement but NOT time spent. Remember you can work for 3 hours or half an hour on something, depending how much pressure you put yourself under. Reward yourself for achieving the milestones and not for the hours put in. You don't want to reward unproductive time.

5.5 Get a TED Injection

Just as you can benefit from the morale boost provided by your public (friends, family, colleagues) you can also get one from watching a short inspirational video.

TED Talks (and the affiliated TEDx sessions) are short 15-20 minute talks delivered by all sorts of people from scientists, sports people, psychologists, entertainers, and public speakers, on many different topics. They embody the ethos of Parkinson's Law by being restricted in duration. They are rich in great content and are in short, bite-sized chunks. Perfect for you as a really busy goal-chaser.

These TED talks are given at events around the world and are posted on the internet for anyone to benefit from, for free. There is a TED channel on some digital platforms in the UK and probably other countries too.

You can search for topics or speakers of interest and then press play.

20 minutes later I guarantee you'll have been educated, entertained and inspired. I don't recall watching any TED talk and not feeling like I'm a little bit better informed afterwards. I almost always finish them feeling inspired.

When you have a natural break in your day, kick back and watch a TED talk. It'll give you an injection of inspiration and energy to keep on going.

Who knows, maybe one day, with all the things you're achieving you could apply to give a TEDx talk. Now there's a big hairy goal to keep you motivated and moving.

6 PERSON

There's only one of you and you're probably wanted and needed by a load of different people. Partner, children, parents, friends, boss, colleagues. And somehow you've decided to reach for a goal or two to accelerate your performance.

If your body or mind are not working properly though you'll let yourself, and those who rely on and value you, down. It is so important to focus on you, the person at the centre of your new high-achieving world.

Rest, sleep, doing good, being happy, loving, and being loved are critical. What's the point of it all if you can't look after yourself in the process.

It's about balance and working out how to achieve your goals while being part of the human race. I advocate going on holiday…..I mean actually ignoring your work and work colleagues while you recharge. I'm a firm believer in proper sleep. Of ignoring the phone. Of blocking out the noise of life when you can (refer back to Section 2 on Distraction).

If you achieve your goals and burn your loved ones in the process, or burn yourself out, you've achieved something that no-one will really care about. If you're burned out, you may end up resenting it. If you burn your friends and family then they will resent your achievement, and maybe even resent you. In fact, they may not see it as much of an achievement.

You. You are the most important thing to look after and we've got a load of tips to help you do what you need, and want, without burning anyone.

6.1 Positive Charging

Achieving goals is best done when awake. Steps toward your goals require Action. Action requires energy, and energy is a finite resource.

Managing your energy so that you feel as good as possible and can attack your To Do list with vigour is one of the most important personal focus areas to be attentive to. There are 86,400 seconds in every 24-hour day. How we use them is important if we're to have a healthy, happy, fulfilled, and high-achieving life. Apart from other things you have to get done in any one day, the other determinant of how much you will achieve is down to how much energy you have.

We all have the ability to manipulate energy, using it to our advantage. If we need a bit of an extra lift we can turn to caffeine, or sugar. Adrenalin also works well. But with these artificial stimulators there's a corresponding low energy trough that follows. That's one of the reasons people get hooked on coffee or sweets, to get through an average day. It's why some people are adrenalin junkies. The high is amazing so let's have that again, and again, and again, until it becomes normal and there's a need to find another more intense high.

In order to deliver consistently it is far better to think about your energy like a battery in a Tesla (other electric cars are available). It's going to run longer if you're not seriously heavy-footed off the lights. It'll run longer if you average a slightly lower speed and don't speed up and down too frequently. When you're running low you look for a charging point and plug in. The car rests and waits for its new energy to accumulate before it can head off again.

So it is for us, our fuels being sleep, food, and oxygen (which is why regular exercise is so important).

It's crucial to get a good night's sleep, but it can also be a really good idea to take a rest during the day. A study conducted in America showed that those who are a bit more Mediterranean and sleep during the day are able to sustain higher average energy levels and improve their output.

While the standard office environment doesn't lend itself to taking a nap at your desk, I have, in the past, headed out to the carpark, got in and had a short 15 minute doze before heading back in for the busy-ness to continue.

Have a think about your energy levels. When do they dip during the day? When are you at your most alert and awesome? Try to schedule your work to match your own daily cycle. And if you need a rest see if you can go and find somewhere to sleep for 20 minutes. This could transform your energy levels and really boost your performance.

6.2 The Early Bird

Are you a morning person? Or do you take forever to get going, preferring instead to work late? Do you both hate mornings and working late? That's allowed. I'm not that keen on either.

There's a debate that rages between the Larks and Night Owls about which approach is best.

Those who rise early advocate that this is the best way to get stuff done. They'll crow that they've done a full day's work before lunch time, and that the rest of the day is then a bonus to be even more productive. They just can't understand why the lazy, work-shy night owls can't see that this is so much better a way to live.

The late risers think the early birds are way too uptight. And so smug. And boring. After all, they go to bed so early, just when the world is really starting to wake up. They'll say they can have peace and quiet to focus when it's quieter at night.

Who's right? It really depends on your biological predisposition.

However, here are some interesting facts from a 2019 survey in the US.

Early birds get 7 hours of sleep a night on average and have sex three times a week. They earn more money and get a better quality of sleep. They tend to be happy, friendly and confident.

Night owls get around 6 hours of sleep a night which is generally of less good quality. They earn less and are shy, tending towards perfectionism. They have sex an average of twice a week.

I have to say that based on this analysis I'm opting for being an early bird. More sleep, more sex and more money! Not necessarily in that order.

Is it possible to change from night owl to early bird? The answer is yes. While it's unlikely that a night owl will suddenly become someone who voluntarily leaps out of bed to go for a run at 4.30am it is possible to shift the time window.

The important thing is to do it bit by bit. Set your alarm to wake 15 minutes earlier and set a bed time 15 minutes earlier. Then repeat. And repeat again.

"Rubbish", a night owl may cry. But think about it. If you fly to another time zone, you're able to adapt through the jet lag to the new time paradigm. So, it IS possible to adapt. The question is how to do it in a way that will be straight forward to achieve.

Research says that those who get up earlier and seize the day get more done. If you're serious about accelerating towards you goals then you might want to consider adapting to be an early bird, if you're not lucky enough to be one already.

6.3 Brrrrrr....Invigorating

Here's a tip that I am almost certain most of you will react with "Think I'll give that a miss!" But I'm including it anyway because it might just be something that at certain times gives you the boost you need.

Cold showers. Yep. Cold showers.

I can feel you shivering at the mention of them. But there are health benefits as well as short-term improvements. You know that feeling, on a beach in the baking sun, overheating as you sip the 3rd Mojito of the afternoon. You dance down to the water's edge trying to avoid burning the soles of your feet on the scorching sand. You feel the instant relief of the colder sea water on your sizzling toes. Then you splash down, burying your shoulders in the water. Which feels Freezing! But by Jove does it feel good for a while. Out you get and the water evaporates from your skin quicker than a Dyson hand dryer can strip your hands of any moisture.

I know it doesn't feel quite like that in the middle of winter when the central heating is on full blast and the water really is blooming freezing when it falls from the shower head, but it's just as good for you and very refreshing.

There's something called the Wim Hof method, which advocates the use of cold for long-term health benefits. You can search it out and see they advocate lying in a bath of ice. That's taking it a bit far for me, but the idea of a cold shower is sometimes great.

There are claims that a cold shower helps to reduce stress levels by increasing stress on the body in the short term and thus making the recipient a little bit hardened towards it. Regular exposure to the cold can increase the white blood cell count and help with immunity. It can stimulate your metabolic rate and so potentially help with weight maintenance or loss. But for me, the most significant benefit is that it's such an excruciating shock to the system that it really wakes me up.

Whenever you're feeling a little bit dull and need a short, sharp energy lift, take a cold shower. You'll suddenly feel very alert, and in the regular partaking of this evil ritual you'll be doing a world of good for your health.

Are you hard enough to take on this challenge??

6.4 Smile For The Camera

Do you find it easier to achieve things when you feel happy or sad, excited or angry? Unless you're a writer, musician or actor who needs to channel the sadness or anger into a poignant verse or performance it's usually best to be in a good, happy, positive frame of mind.

If you're not really feeling it today, is there a way to change your frame of mind and get in a happier place? If you could you'd not only do better work towards your goals but you'll also simply feel a bit better about life and yourself.

The key is to wear a genuine and infectious smile every day.

A study conducted in 2011 by the University of Aberdeen found that people rated those who made eye contact and smiled as more attractive than those who did not. We all like a good smile because they make us feel good. Another study found that seeing someone smile activates the part of the brain that processes sensory reward. Science tells us that receiving smiles makes the world more attractive and makes us feel really good.

Imagine if you smile at the world. How good are you going to make others feel? Complete strangers, friends, colleagues, family. That in itself is a good enough reason to do it. Doing good things for others is very rewarding (see section 6.5). And, if you make others feel good they are more likely to want to do something for you when it's time for you to delegate a task that they could do and isn't so important to you.

But how does smiling make the smiler feel?

Smiling activates areas of your brain, releasing neuropeptides which enable neurons to communicate. Neuro-transmitters such as dopamine, serotonin, and endorphins are released, giving a happy boost. Stress can feel like it's washing away and the body relaxes as the heart rate lowers. These natural chemicals can do for you what a prescription from the doctor could do, only without the possible side effects.

A smile is free, has no bad side effects, will make you look more attractive, and it will make you feel better.

When you wake in the morning imagine you're that favourite film star, musicians, or television presenter who has a killer smile which melts your heart. Then, smile for the camera and take on the world.

6.5 Do Good For The Hell Of It

In the mid-2000s I read a book called 'Random Acts of Kindness' by Danny Wallace. There are 365 suggestions for random acts that could make someone's day. Some of them are very funny:

1. Bellow a cheery hello to a vicar or a nun
2. Give a slice of your pizza to the delivery man
3. Phone someone in a call centre and tell them they're doing a great job
4. There's even one about buying a pack of cigars and leaving them at the maternity ward for the new fathers!

I'm not sure some of them actually work, but with 365 to choose from there are bound to be some that you would look at and say "I could do that!"

I found the book pretty inspiring. In fact, it's now a whole movement. Did you know that 3 days after Valentine's day, on 17th February every year it is Random Acts of Kindness Day, promoted by the Random Acts of Kindness Foundation. Who knew there was such a thing?

There are benefits to being kind above making others feel really special which can have a knock on impact to how they treat you or how karma touches you. There are benefits to you as the giver of kind actions, such as:

> 1. One study found that people feel stronger and more energetic after helping others
> 2. A Harvard Business School survey showed that those who help others are happier than those who don't
> 3. Helping others can release serotonin, the happy chemical, which can reduce stress and make you calmer
> 4. Doing things for others triggers the reward centre in your brain giving the giver a 'high'
> 5. Another study found that those who volunteer have a significantly lower likelihood of dying younger
> 6. Oxytocin, the love hormone, is released increasing self-esteem and optimism
> 7. Kind people have a lower level of cortisol which is also known as the stress hormone
> 8. It can help reduce anxiety and depression with the release of serotonin
> 9. Oxytocin also keeps blood pressure lower

Just by randomly being kind to others you will improve your mood and your health (and likability!) which in turn will help you achieve your goals.

You will also help to make the world a nicer and kinder place.

6.6 Phones Are Not Great Bedfellows

When my eldest daughter got her first phone we were naturally worried that she'd have access to lots of websites, chat apps and other things that could be unsavoury. We put in place the best possible filtering software on the WiFi network, and restricted her phone to certain apps and content types online.

Even though this was a good way to protect her and give us piece of mind it wasn't quite all we did. The other concern was that if she had her phone in her room at night she'd find a reason to be on it. Even if we restricted her use of the WiFi at night, she'd still be able to use her mobile data.

So, we removed temptation and made a rule that the phone would not be allowed in her bedroom from lights off to morning. The phone would be plugged in to charge downstairs and she'd be able to use it again the next day.

What benefits would this bring? Better sleep. Less anxiety about missing out on 'important' social media stuff, an appreciation of boundaries, and not forming a mobile phone addiction from day one.

It's easy to impose rules for a child (we did get some pushback initially but largely it was fine and became the accepted norm) but it's a lot harder to change our own behaviour if we've been used to having our electronic appendages ever present by our sides while we sleep.

I was talking to someone recently who asked her children for an alarm clock for a birthday present. This she would use instead of her phone's alarm for wake up time. The idea of receiving this as a gift from treasured children is that it'd make her more likely to use it on a daily basis. And, she has. Her phone now lives downstairs while she gets a significantly better quality of sleep without the potential for distraction.

I accept this is not going to be high on the priority list of many of you making a change towards higher productivity but it's one that, if it's good enough for the kids, is surely good enough for us.

6.7 Ditch the Screen and Sleep Like a Baby

There's a lot of evidence to suggest that artificial light impacts our circadian rhythm. Too much of it late at night, or just before going to sleep, can have a negative effect on your ability to fall asleep. The strength of the light and its colour have an impact.

The lower the strength the better. And the less white it is, the less stimulation. In white light, or natural light, there are a lot of blue wavelengths and it is these that are thought to be harmful to your chances of dropping off quickly at night. This is why the mobile manufacturers have different light settings for evening or night time that filter out the blue. If you turn on 'night mode' the screen will go a little yellowy because the blue has been removed.

Applying this filter when you're reading an article, or browsing social media is okay. But, do you really want a yellow tinge as you watch an episode of 'Killing Eve'? Probably not. It just wouldn't look quite right or convey the intended dramatic emotions.

The wisdom out there suggests that it's the two factors of light strength and colour which have the most impact, though there is another that I think is key. The content on the screen.

Watching an episode of 'Luther' just before you intend to sleep just isn't the best preparation for a calm and easy descent into the blissful semi-conscious state of sleep. With your heart racing and brain whirring as it goes back over what just happened, there's a little time needed to recover.

Reading through the latest opinion piece from the Mail Online might similarly set you off on a bit of a head spin. Quickly looking something up which you've been meaning to do for a while then inevitably leads you to check something else, and then another thing. The brain is alive and awake. What about checking Facebook or Instagram? Your receptors will be firing and making connections.

You get the point. All of these things are stimulating, regardless of the light quality itself.

Ditch your screens before bedtime and get into a peaceful, uncluttered, restful state to maximise your chances of nodding off more quickly.

6.8 Block the Noise Out

If you have to work in an open plan office then I offer you my sincere condolences. While they can be fun at times as the banter flows and you temporarily feel the warm glow of love for your colleagues (even the normally very irritating one), they can be bloody distracting.

As you settle down to your action list, needing to concentrate and give it your all to finish by the deadline, you're aware of the conversation being held at full volume over in the corner about how the dog needs to go in for grooming or the green fees at some overpriced golf course in Buckinghamshire are rather steep. Somehow, the harder you try to block this irrelevant stuff out the louder it seems to get.

Then there's the sales guy with absolutely no emotional intelligence who shouts across your desk to the person sitting next to you about what he needs them to do for his customer. He calls out to another sales guy about the awesome night they had 'drinking it large' with their customers last night.

Like you needed to know that!

I'm all for a bit of fun and bonding with colleagues, but there's a time and a place for it which is not at top volume across a crowded open plan office.

The solution is to work from home or in a meeting room, but assuming those aren't options, headphones.

Even if you aren't listening to music, which we'll come on to in the next section, but simply want a bit of peace and quiet, headphones are the answer.

And categorically not those little ear buds that hang from inside your ears. Why? Because no-one can see them unless they are standing right next to you.

No! You need the biggest, most obvious over-ear headphones that scream "Back off. Leave me alone. I'm having some me time and focusing on becoming awesome." Most people will think twice about disturbing you if you wear them.

If you can afford some noise cancelling headphones from Bose or the like, I'd recommend them. They won't completely eradicate all sound but they'll muffle it so much that you'll feel like you're in your own world.

No noise means you can focus on getting the job done pronto.

6.9 Music but No Rap

There's something called 'neuromusicology'. It looks at how our nervous system reacts to music. Music activates a number of different areas of the brain and these vary from person to person. Largely it depends on the type of training and interaction the person has had with music as to how many of the areas get lit up.

Despite these individual differences there are some common things that seem to affect us all. Research has shown that music can reduce confusion and delirium in patients and that if we listen to sad or happy music it can influence whether we perceive people to be sad or happy. This is a well understood phenomenon that's used by film and television programme makers as they seek to influence our emotions during a drama.

A study from 2012 suggests that creativity increases with ambient noise (meaning music) in the background if played at a moderate volume. If too loud then creativity plunges. The sound of a flowing stream can improve mood and productivity, apparently (though at my age is more likely to make me want to pee!). Another study from 1999 showed that playing classical or rock music to a group of people enabled them to identify numbers more quickly and accurately than a control group. According to the Journal of the American Medical Association music increases the accuracy and efficiency of surgeons. Next time you are in for an operation ask the surgeon what they're going to listen to while they poke around performing their cut-and-slice magic.

There's a bit of a debate about whether music with words has a beneficial or detrimental impact on levels of productivity and focus. One school of thought says that words stimulate the brain and therefore they can be distracting while trying to concentrate. Therefore if the task you're trying to undertake is reasonably taxing it is probably best to avoid music with lyrics.

If, on the other hand, the work is relatively repetitive and mundane, studies have shown that songs with lyrics can be beneficial, possibly because the words provide some relief from the boring and mind-numbing tasks being performed.

Whatever works for you is the right type of music. Try different genres and see how they impact your focus, concentration, and productivity.

6.10 Out Of The Bunker

Where do you do your best work? Where do you do most of your work? Whenever you want to be highly productive you should set about the tasks where you feel the best and most productive.

If you work in a dark environment with little natural light on a regular basis you could be doing yourself a major disservice.

Dr. Alan Hedge from Cornell University conducted a study and found that optimising natural light in the work environment led to a 51% drop in the incidences of eye strain, a drop of 63% in headaches, and a 56% reduction in drowsiness. Now, tell me, are you likely to be at your best and most alert or creative if you have a headache or are feeling drowsy?

It makes sense, purely based on those statistics, to work from a place which has the most amount of natural light possible.

I know that when I worked from the offices of one company I would get home after a full day and be absolutely exhausted. The meeting rooms were windowless and stuffy. No natural light and not a lot of fresh air, which is another key thing that research has pointed to as being a booster for productivity. We all need fresh air.

Interestingly, a survey of 1,614 working adults conducted in North America by Future Workplace revealed that the number one employee perk people crave is a working environment with natural light. This beat the desire to have a restaurant, gym, or childcare.

Wherever you plan to work, make sure it it somewhere with plenty of natural light. You will feel better and will perform at a much higher level.

6.11 Small + Often = Habit

All the tips, tools and tricks in the world aren't going to 'make' you more productive in the long run. They will help you be more focused and efficient. They will get you to take action and tap into your motivation.

But it's only when you 'become' the different person, the more productive version of yourself that it will last forever.

You need to think about making productivity a habit, something you do so frequently that it becomes automatic. Habits take time to form and it is in the frequency and consistency of application that they stick.

The first step is to actually implement some of the suggestions in this book. If you simply read them and think they make sense but never apply them then you'll not achieve a great deal more than you are right now. Do them often and over a long period of time to make them stick.

Try not to make the initial changes too big. Don't try and implement all 67 tips from this book on day one. You will fail and rather than helping you you'll find that nothing really works and you'll stop, saying that the book was crap and didn't help you.

Take a few of the elements in the book and consciously decide to implement them for a week, and then another week, and another two, until you've consistently done them every day for at least 4-6 weeks.

The key is to make some of these things habits, and it's through making good new habits that you'll really see an acceleration towards being a productive ninja.

Become the person you want to be. One good new habit at a time.

6.12 Up-skill

"Education is the passport to the future, for tomorrow belongs to those who prepare for it today." So said Malcolm X. And so say parents the world over to their children when they don't focus in school (some kind of variant of this, at least).

Learning is a privilege, expands the mind and is fun. Those who continue to learn keep fresh minds, open to new possibilities and things they didn't know or understand before. In my view, learning is something we should all keep doing as it helps to advance us as people and drives a greater collective knowledge and understanding.

My mother is in her mid-seventies and is seemingly never not on a course of some kind. She has an insatiable interest in lots of things; health, wellbeing, and nutrition being at the top of the list. She is so alert and interested. Consequently she is also very interesting. If any of her friends have questions about those topics she's the first person they call, knowing they'll get a helpful answer from a really knowledgeable person.

Learning keeps my mother young.

In addition to it being good for you, learning can also help you accelerate toward your goals faster. There may be a skill that you don't currently possess that would significantly help you.

Say, for example, you want to be able to cook like a celebrity chef, knowing how to chop your onions or carrots quickly and without the need to reach for the blue plasters to patch up bleeding fingers would be a useful skill to learn. If your ambition is to run a sub 3hr30m marathon you might think about learning as much as you can about nutrition and recovery so that your hours out pounding the streets can be put to best use. If you're bidding on a significant piece of business with a client and you're likely to need to present the solution and pricing to their board you'd be well advised to undertake a presentation skills course to give yourself the best possible shot at winning.

Think about your current skill levels and the tasks you're going to need to complete as you reach for your goals, then write down the areas where you might want to up-skill yourself. And, just like any of your goals, make sure you then create a comprehensive list of actions/process steps to enable you to achieve the up-skilling goal.

6.13 Patience is a Virtue

You've set your ultimate goals, defined your process steps/actions and are ploughing through them. But it feels like you're not really making progress fast enough. You've taken the time to be clear about what you want to achieve and are feeling a bit frustrated about how long it's taking. Now that you're a goal setting, action orientated ninja you want results and you want them NOW!

Don't fret. It's a really common feeling.

You may also feel a little overwhelmed as there are still a whole load of process steps to take and you can't see your way through them to get to the end.

It can be disheartening. But don't let the magnitude of your ambitions overwhelm you and get you down.

To achieve anything of any significance takes real effort and application. It takes time.

To master anything takes 10,000 hours of practice according to Malcolm Gladwell in his excellent book

'Outliers'. That means to master a musical instrument (real mastery of it), for example, would require 20 hours a week for 10 years before you'd have really nailed it.

The good news is that you don't need to spend as much time as that heading for your goals. But you do need to spend quite a few hours in a consistent way to move forwards.

When I started running I was overweight, asthmatic and really very lazy. My youthful days of rowing glory(ish) were decades past. I ran 1km and nearly died. Then stretched it a bit. And some more. If I'd thought about the full extent of running 42.2km in one go without stopping I'd easily have been disheartened.

I have daughters who each learn multiple musical instruments. They work methodically through the grades and eventually go for Grade 8 (or reluctantly with much screaming and shouting some days). If they focused on Grade 8 straight away they (and we!) would probably give up. It just seems a mountain to climb.

The thing to remember is that you're only aiming to hit the next milestone (process step) along the route to achieving your goal. If you've mapped out the steps and given them deadlines and an overall timeframe you'll be able to see how long it'll take to get to where you want to be.

You must be patient. Just tick off the tasks and move on to the next. In the words of Arianna Grande 'thank u, next."

6.14 Holiday Properly

A former colleague and friend of mine runs a busy marketing department in a very large global telecoms company. I used to sail with him a lot and we entered a few running races together. In fact, he's to blame for my dodgy knees.

On one cold, grey and damp March day sailing on the Solent I'd been lamenting the fact that every holiday I'd taken in the past few years had been punctuated by work escalations. I was running a global organisation at the time and there was a lot going on.

He just looked at me and asked, "Why do you take your laptop with you?"
I stuttered and replied, "Because I need to."
"Says who?' he probed.
"I just need to."
"That's your choice then," he concluded.

He was really clear with his team and his boss that when he was on holiday he was gone from the business. He made sure the right people were in place and empowered to make decisions in his absence. And no-one ever needed to escalate to him.

I learned a valuable lesson from him and decided from that day forward to adopt the same approach.

There are three benefits:
1. I really get to recharge without worrying about office stuff
2. My family gets 100% of me for the few precious weeks a year I can do this - and they deserve to be treated properly, just like I do
3. My team understands how to take responsibility and accountability for things without always referring back to me

I urge you to look after yourself, your family, and team, and really go on holiday. You all deserve it, and you'll end up being so much more productive once you get back. Your battery will be back to 100% full charge, rather than a rather tired 80%.

6.15 Don't be a Weekend Warrior

Have you had a boss who sends emails out to their team on the weekend with asks for information or actions? I have been on the receiving end of these and they always made me feel a bit jumpy. Under pressure. "They've sent this on the weekend so it must be urgent. I'd better reply now."

If you receive something like this and decide to respond you'll spend your precious weekend time on something that 99% guaranteed could have waited until Monday morning. That's time away from your own passions, hobbies and family to answer something that is unlikely to have been needed on a Sunday!

I'm ashamed to say that I'm guilty of having done this to my teams in the past. I now try to avoid it if at all possible.

If you're working on a client tender that has a deadline of 9am Monday morning then it's fine to work with the team over the weekend, as long as everyone is agreed that's what you're all going to do. (Although, having said that, if you implement some of the smart productivity tips in this book you may find it's all completed by the previous Friday).

What I'm suggesting is that you should avoid sending out unsolicited and unnecessary emails to anyone. By all means draft the email but don't send it until it needs to land in their inbox.

Ultimately it's about treating others how you'd like to be treated yourself at the same time as being sure whether something is both important and urgent.

7 WHAT NEXT?

Now that you have read through these 67 ways to improve your focus and productivity more quickly than ever, the next step is to put some of them into practice.

Take action today. Choose a few and begin to make them part of your daily routine.

Your success will be determined by your ability to turn these suggestions into habits. Look back at the section called "Small + Often = Habit" (6.11) to refresh yourself on how to create good new habits.

Remember we set a challenge in "Actually do these for 30 days" (4.7).

Now's the time to increase your productivity and I'd like to hear how you get on. Visit us at accelerate-performance.com/feedback60 to leave feedback.

If you're interested in learning more about how to form good new habits and achieve the goals you want to, faster, you can read my new book "Accelerate Personal Performance". It's filled with more really useful stuff that's based on scientific evidence (so it really does work) and

stories (who doesn't love a good story?) about notable successes. For more information visit:
accelerate-performance.com/books/accelerate-personal-performance

"Accelerate Personal Performance" is a must read for anyone interested in knowing:

- How to create your own luck
- The importance of defining your purpose
- The importance of networking
- How, why and when to delegate
- How to be an amazing influencer
- How to set goals that you'll stick to
- How to break old bad habits and form brilliant new ones
- How to become mentally tough and disciplined
- How to overcome blocks

Visit accelerate-performance.com/books for more information.

8 CAN YOU DO ME A FAVOUR?

If you've enjoyed this book and it's helped you in some way please can you do me a favour and write a review on Amazon?

If you do you'll be helping accelerate the book's performance as well as enabling loads of other people to benefit from the FEDAMP Productivity Model with its 67 ideas (that's a whole 10 more than Heinz's Varieties - what a bargain!).

Just think of posting a review as a random act of kindness You'll be doing good just for the hell of it.

Please visit accelerate-performance.com/feedback60 and leave a review on the Accelerate Performance website or go to Amazon and leave one there. If you're feeling amazingly generous, how about both? I'd be enormously grateful.

Thank you very much in advance.

9 MORE AT ACCELERATE PERFORMANCE

You might have bought this book because you found Accelerate Performance first. Or you might have found us from Amazon, or elsewhere.

Wherever you stumbled upon this book remember there are lots of articles, tips and tricks at Accelerate Performance. Find us at accelerate-performance.com

If you have any comments or extra ideas to take this guide from 67 to a higher number (can we get to 100?) let me know.

You can email me at info@accelerate-performance.com or leave feedback at:
accelerate-performance.com/feedback60

Thank you for buying and virtual hugs for reading.

ABOUT THE AUTHOR

Ralph Varcoe is an author, musician, and highly experienced business leader who has spent way too many years building businesses and teams.

From taking a mail order book business to being a publisher while still at college, creating an online community and social network for the boating community, working as a consultant in multiple technology companies, driving sales and marketing growth through Europe and beyond, building sales strategies and teams to deliver value to customers globally, to acting as a business mentor for entrepreneurs and start-ups, Ralph has a wealth of experience in what it takes to perform at the top level, and guide others to do the same.

He is a trained singer, having performed classical and jazz at venues from London to Shanghai, and writes and records songs for fun. He is an avid sailor, having skippered his team to 1st place in a number of regattas, and is passionate about giving women a greater and more valued position in the working world. He has a partner, with four daughters between them, and lives in Hampshire, UK.